ironclad

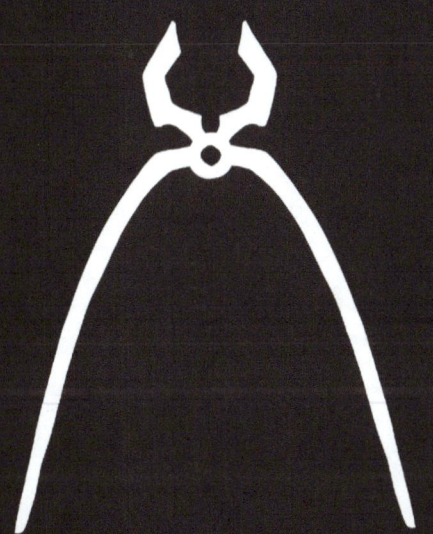

marc vincenz

illustrated by jake quatt

ironclad
the future present

ir⌀nclad
the future present

marc vincenz

illustrated by jake quatt

spuyten duyvil

Cover design, book design, typography, concept, words,
tonics, steels and sonics by Marc Vincenz.

Cover and back cover images:
"Slotted Steel & Chains," 2024, by Jake Quatt.

All archeological artifact artwork by Jake Quatt.

The Mayfly Codex appeared as a limited edition folio with Spuyten Duyvil, NYC, 2024.

A small selection of these works entitled from Ironclad appeared as a digital chapbook published
by Mudlark: An Electronic Journal of Poetry & Poetics (University of North Florida, 2024).

Printed and bound in the United States of America.

ISBN 978-1-963908-88-6

Library of Congress Control Number: 2025942937

From the whetted lips of a prophet,
every single word is ironclad.

ARCHAEOLOGICAL STRATIFICATION

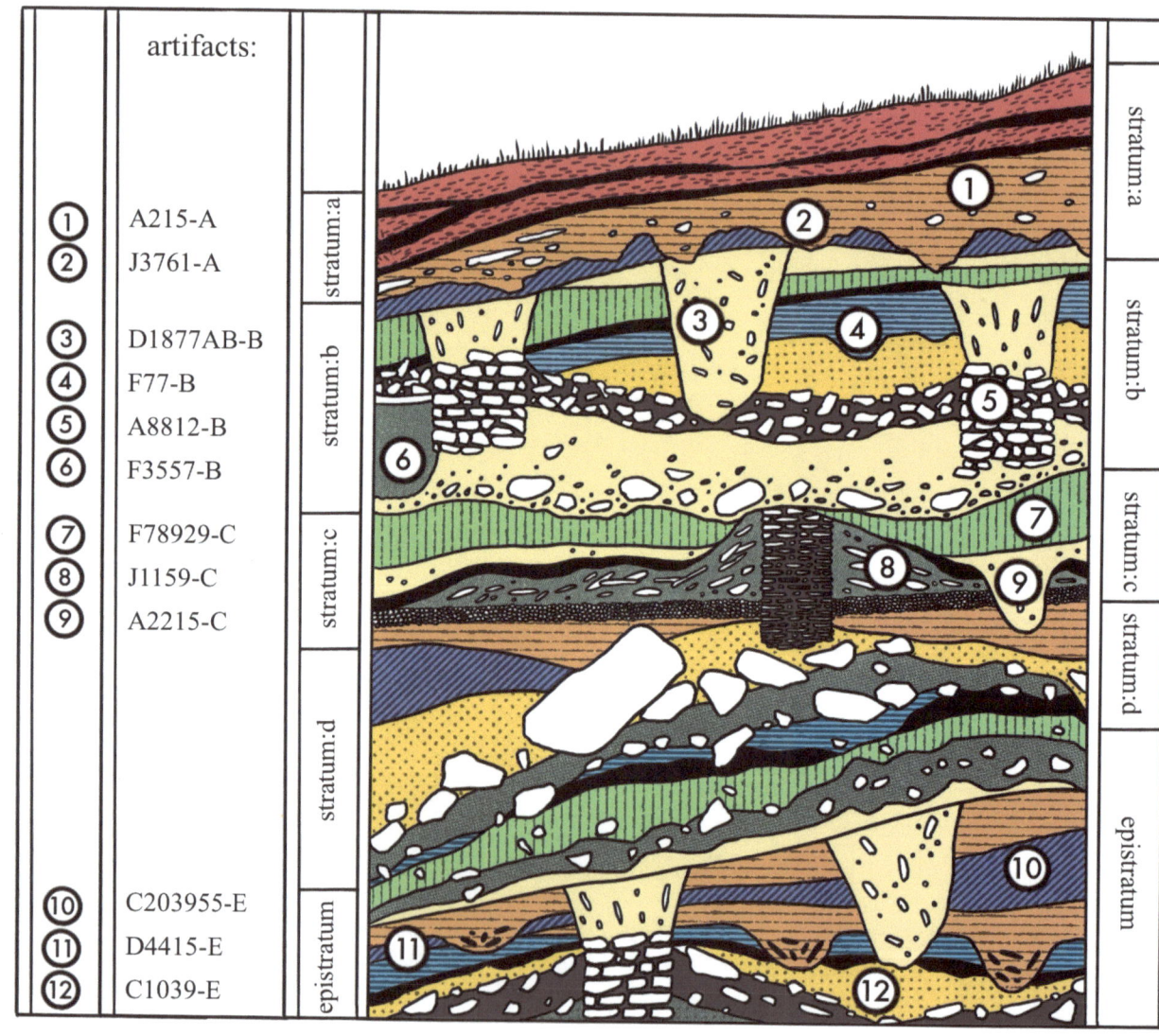

artifacts:

①	A215-A
②	J3761-A
③	D1877AB-B
④	F77-B
⑤	A8812-B
⑥	F3557-B
⑦	F78929-C
⑧	J1159-C
⑨	A2215-C
⑩	C203955-E
⑪	D4415-E
⑫	C1039-E

stratum:a

stratum:b

stratum:c

stratum:d

epistratum

stratum:a

stratum:b

stratum:c

stratum:d

epistratum

x

STRATUM B:
a house of mirth

STRATUM D:
a common wheel, a common prayer

The Enchanted Codex
of the Peoples
of Ø

EPISTRATUM:
a prophet is born
somewhere else
every other day

A Few Thoughts on the Texts & Fragments

How to elucidate the feelings aroused by this hapless archeologist & sometime filmmaker, & recently appointed Commissioner of the Iron Plier Society? Well, terrified! Sweating profusely on the under-lip, carrion birds circling, an electric storm gathering: a faint quivering of the ancestor's voices, as they say back in the old country.

We have finally succeeded in sifting through the distant past; in these pages, in the very least, you'll feel a semblance of the emotions pumping through the wrists of your own progenitors. For centuries we have grappled with the concept of what residue trailed behind. How the senses were manifested in the cosmic tides & the cognitive apparition that was more confined to the tantalizing realm of the quantum. Modern science has simplified these tasks dramatically. We wish to thank the Universities of New Netherlandia, Trottelheim Zwei & Ossettia B, Professors Smythe-Listerman & Abydon-Festerman from the Society of Iron Culture & Practical Understanding, & for the Commissioner General of Information & Bright Insight of our own illuminated city.

Many of us had a whiff of the breadcrumb trail that would lead us to the End Movement & the Containment, & have persevered just as the holy twinned ravens & their sister serpent.

Which prior citizen had deposited the Great Idea in the dusty medium of the soaring Ash Cloud? For every major innovation is next in a generation of further cognitive eruptions, or so sayeth the Great Smith, plowing ahead with her fabulous Solar Irons.

Dear citizens, in seventeen & a half years we have unearthed tens of millions of cubic hands of organic & inorganic matter. That leap across millennia is a mere blink—almost as if your ancestor had turned back to face you eye to eye—& in that briefest fluttering of fingers or that sideways glance, handed you all their civil dreams, their savage inspirations & caustic aspirations.

Please peruse these chambers & walls & little-known alcoves with an open mind, & know despite the eons they divide, the fathers & mothers they served are almost the same as you & I.

May we all find our misnomers in the dark & spell them out in an illuminating firelight, & may the union of Father Fire & Mother Oil enflame us all.

Intrepidly, ever-cognitively, & as fiercely practical as always, your,

Citizen-Smythe Frederica Faustina-Flysson, ☉ ••
Chairperson for the Society for the Preservation of Iron & Oil, City of New Ø

STRATUM A:

a misnomer

Time
& truth

infuse
your

spinal
cord

with an
im-

mu-
table

sense
of lightness.

[•] prelumination

An Earthly Archeologist Does Her Very Best

& in her youth, as was the fashion of her aquatic ancestors, she dined on sea snails, periwinkles, mealy clams, clusters of limp seaweeds, seed shrimp & briny sea grasses, & these sustained her like a weathered river-vane sensing her currents—

even through that uneven breathing as she wrestled anointed roots of copperwood tree upon copperwood tree upcountry terrestrially from valley to sea, replanting them in the dirt which was the place that begat our great mother city—

6

Or So the Ancient Saying Goes:

Arm in arm,
the fragrance

of copperwood
attends you

through hill
& dale, along

well-worn
wormweed trails,

just as one godly
eye follows you in-

to the steady,
steely storm:

We feed off
each other, silently,

was once said
quite quietly.

[••] of birth & space & time & light

ǀ

The Myth of Ø

Trees Trees Trees

On a walkabout with her conscience, an old woman
wanders the savanna dragging an old tree, sweeping up dust.
Copperwood: a balm for the soul, she heaves & sighs & coughs.

Let me help you, let me carry your burden, says Ø passing by.
No, young woman, mine alone to carry! says the old woman.
Ø trips on a rock, dances among the roots of an ancient tree

as if the sky were falling, but rights her surer footing.
You carry your own burden too, says the old woman wheezing.
& mine to carry alone, says Ø, palms on her knees deep-breathing.

A mind is much to carry, says the old woman, & proceeds to hoist
the old tree upon her shoulders; tawdry leaves tangle in her wiry hair,
until, to be fair, the weight falls upon her, & drives her down

through the surface beneath the earthworms—where, accordingly,
the earth herself recounts another story of fire & brimstone,
of theft & burden, & the rise & fall & rise of the surface-bound:

all the palm fronds splayed in virtuousness or clasped in prayer,
& so too the wiry fingers, who fall upon heavy shoulders.
Ø picks up the old tree, hoists it to her very own & walks on.

10

Twinned Ravens, a Plea

A minor mirror of twinned resplendent creatures:
a major discourse cut between two of the same cloth:
an infernal debate concerning those who were not at hand:

When the island is seen, a vast luxuriating green—
the cheers resound from here to the old motherland, &
our two young ravens are returning from the shore:

It has been sighted! they call out, & the people break out
in *vino veritas*, empty every flagon & flask in sight, raise glasses
& spirits, & flutes & mandolins serenade the night.

& eventually, we strike land, drag heels through sands,
until upon a clearing bright in the midst of a cloud forest,
the sun breaks through to reveal a tree stump with the face

of an old woman: That's her conscience, a girl with braids says.
Her mother, an old woman too, scolds: Shame on you, child!
The tribal leader says: a good place to plant ourselves.

We need to live in a place with a conscience, a place where we carry
our own burden with no shoulders to fall upon, even in prayer.
Meanwhile, the spirit of Ø observes from a wooded incline.

O Plus O Plus O Plus One Equals ⊘

& thus, by imperial decree, with the flourish of one hand,
the new world was born on the seashore & the edge of the jungle,
among the crabs & caiman & the five-eyed newts.

& such she was, Woman of the Holy Serpent: born, it was said,
from the hot bosom of the volcano among the New & Forgiven,
here at the face in the stump, where the old woman's conscience

was once again, one eye arched, hairy nostrils flared, reprimanding—
right here at the heart of the city! where, this very morning
goatherds strolled the abundant inclines, vendors plied their wares,

each & every fish glimmering, each fruit in plentitude—mangoes
brisling to the size of melons & blood oranges bleeding like coconuts;
crustaceans & crabs of every hue of pink & red—&,

here too was where the Woman of the Holy Serpent entwined
with the twinned ravens & a mycelium now known to be the root
of the decline of a civilization; here we chose to raise our city!

Let them all stare! Let them point fingers! Let them throw stones!
& thus, by imperial decree, with the flourish of one hand,
the new world was born on the seashore at the edge of the jungle.

12

Fragments of a City Called Ø in Linear B

A21-3B: broken wax seal, tooth marks

Earthen hills of dirt, & sand & broken bones
& smashed pottery guard the city; a long line of vendors
assembles on the first vestiges of muddy streets

& cobbled lanes: the Center Ø, or the Forum, they call it.
Trees are logged, stacked & counted, then shipped off
somewhere even more bountiful where colorful birds

are shot, garroted, plucked, roasted & happily polished off
with lemon rind, shallot, finely sliced turmeric, & Oceanic garlic.
You can purchase delectable birdheart skewers & deep-

fried monkey testicles on almost every corner.
Monkeys too clamor in the trees—& some of them,
the intrepid, leap palm-leaf huts & the tiled inner-city,

& skirt the first muddy channels of the growing sprawl & ooze.
Refuse collects: swirling soups of gray & green
& frothy-spumy-white accumulate fruit fly swarms.

Stirring films of the sheerest plastics
                                             radiate
                                   in brilliant ultraviolets.

A67-1De: unbroken wax seal, fragment torn

Vendors assemble their hard-won wares:
coal, tin & iron ore from the Moss Mountains [...]

[...] parasols from Profusio & pottery
made in the heady stream that was Ruffello [...]

[...] saffron & spices from the Salt Islands,
& snailshells & pearls from the Mother Islands [...]

[...] coral & turquoise from the Purple Umbra of Trottelheim [...]

A344-17H: broken wax seal, scratches, thumbprint

The faithful & the faithless converged …

upon the new city square, which was not yet quite square …

[…] the city planners had been at their prints day & night
for weeks & weeks; & the laborers

    (who came from as far afield as Magenticum)

arrived here hoping to find a city plated in gold […]

The planners took note, &
designated an area
on the furthest fringes
of the swamplands
where, on weekends,
immigrants could dig petulantly
to their heart's pulsing lamplights.

A697-3Bc: cracked fragment

[…] from the House of the Heavens,
discover the latest storm […]

Once we filled our teeth with lead, later only vice.

The Crooked Spine of a Holy Serpent

There are some who believe
the world existed before—

in too many incarnations,
long too before that

indescribable miraculous Birth:
the Smiths hinted at it in their ancient,

rusted etchings discovered
on that fateful thirteenth full moon,

generations later, beneath
the cremated ruins of the first Fire Temple;

meanwhile, the temple sages
consolidate their responses;

& in waving their arms generously,
& in generally flimflamming about

in their all-holy & pre-ordained &
endorsed prescriptions & procedures, they sit firm:

The Smiths had always said, be humble:
but be aware, be hawk-eyed:

be also purposeful, be concerted,
be forward-leaning:

there's motivation behind
every action or inaction

no matter how large or small—
suggesting, of course, that

meaning is to be found
in the simplest of things too,

18   even in pounding dirty laundry
on the rocks of an elegant river.

A Thin Pantheon of Demigods

No lines, no marks,
unblemished, firm skin

on purpose; & for those
with a discerning eye, some-

thing extraordinary emerges:
a sad flower who wishes to be

a thunderstorm that dwells within
the day's aches, but finds its way out

into the sunshine: such were the words
& metaphors espoused by the new regime:

all those high cells towering over the rest of us—
such godlike creatures who determined fate, fame,

& loss, who manifested history in her torrential reign.
Still, Sunday evenings in the communal hall, all bets were off.

Tiny Poem of Microverses

For those
in the know:
open

here.

Linear B-2 graffiti on the backboard of a marble bed

The Iron Plier Society

[•] for clutching red-hot tongs

Dutiful to the Last Decree,
such was the Last Pilgrim
upon their Final Pilgrimage:

forged by a local Smith:
the iron pliers were hammered
to extract rusty nails

from a substance far harder
than iron—an element,
harvested with zeal,

for eons by the makers
of racks & other torture contraptions,
of L-shaped, tongue-&-groove

contrivances that wielded nooses
or barbed chains, who silently
raised double-

headed axes in shadows, who
carried out tall orders, &,
executed accordingly.

21

[••] for better a Smith to forge

The Iron Plier Society
was selective, the price
of entry, prohibitive;

yet somehow, young
Frederick Flysson made
the proverbial pinch, & pinched

within an inch of his flesh,
he too was branded
with a caustic searing plier;

& he joked he was now
in the elite herd, among the queens
of fire-breathing horses, & after

having been milked out
of their mercurial elixir,
would settle on any aging pasture,

as long as there were daisies
& buttercups, & whirlybeetles
& wild gujuberries.

[●●●] for whistling while working

&, Grandmaster Flysson,
in his last great year
serving the Cause, decided

from thence forth,
every household
should receive

their own pair of holy pliers:
an instrument gifted
from the Iron Plier Society

23

to look down at you from
your fresh plaster walls,
to accompany you as you work,

to serve you as guardian
of the more-practical self:

[••••] for capricious practical notes

For only as a practical self,
can the self be fulfilled:
so sayeth the Founding Smith

from the Forge of Creation
in candlelight, poring over
their reminiscences & copious

accumulations—for a moment,
estranged they were, far from their
practical self, & in that last

24

thunderstruck second, they awoke
unsure who or what they were,
until gradually, they were melted

into a better version
of their practical self.

[⊙] for the cast-iron will

& like an old fire-breathing horse,
they galloped among the old pastures
where buttercups & ironflowers,

where copperberries & slagbeetles
were all aplenty; &, then, finally,
as their teeth ground down to a nub,

& their taste buds shed their skins,
the eyes too began
to tear uncontrollably;

it was then they cast their bones
upon sacred ground for all &
everyone to devour. Such was

the all-practical self, said they, self-
practicing the less-practical self.

& Then Descended the Wolves

& one night they whooped & howled as they fell upon us from the rubberized hills—forlorn, but, by extending their flexible front paws, endeared themselves to both the townsfolk & the high citizenry—& by leaping through flaming wheels made of dried cornhusks & wildflowers, & by gleefully dancing across waist-high meadows & catching butterflies in their teeth, & through the cobbled lanes of the city bearing life, & by offering tokens of dead & dying mammals, of sea-weed, or crimson pebbles of sea glass & mind-bending, multidimensional fungi we later named the One, they were beloved & adored—& as they nestled in their places by our hearths, from our crumbling plaster walls, the iron pliers of the Holy Smiths clamped down & embraced us all.

Fragment in Linear B-2 in the tomb of Marcus Aesophagus ascribed to the "founding First Smiths" (see List of Semi-Mythological Rulers)

Fragment Seventy-Seven C

Was the burden
of the populace

(at least represented
by their conscience);

(still, apportioned,
conscience can be bought

like many other
convenient things),

(at least, so say
the old folks);

(&, this was realized,
somewhere down the corridor),

(& was passed on
to the corresponding gene),

accordingly.

27

Before the Flood Watch

On such days as when, in
their opinion, the sun lay
low on the beaches,

the coastline rumbled

& bubbled & broiled;
&, for a short minute,
the langoustines could be

finger-plucked well-done

28   from steamy waters.
It was then the heavens
bowled over & doubled in
upon themselves
in a last-ditch effort,
a lone woodpecker touched
the earth with her soft kiss.

Then, one of those Sages tiptoed by
carrying their dirty laundry,
& said: There are dead
birds simply everywhere.

Bleeding Crown of Thorns

Don't forget, one mother
once said to her stubborn son:

Don't revert to the mental time travel
you got used to in your youth.

Who doesn't need to know
about their past, someone once asked.

Who doesn't live by time running
on a clock, has often been said.

Can we all sit together at the same spiritual table?
a sage was supposed to have once intoned.

Psychoemotionally you are reacting to a cosmic perspective,
it was once explained as what that spiritual fellow meant.

Otherwise, once, every-
thing else seemed impossible.

Linear B-2 translation from a fresco behind a temple in Ossetia

Tiny Poem on the Dark Ages

Down at the creek,
S finally finds her
tiny shoes. Strangely,
her tiny soles are missing.

Linear B translation on a silver amulet wrapped around a female index finger

Tiny Poem of the Unknown

Who spends less
than five percent
of their time
at the **surface**?

31

Tiny Poem on Improved Sanitary Practices

32

Pliers
could also
be used
to extract
movable

teeth.

Linear B-2 graffiti on the underside of an accountant's iron desk

Tiny Poem on More Improved Sanitary Practices

Pliers
could also
be used
to extract
movable

taxes.

Linear B-2 graffiti inscribed on a dentist's alabaster stool

A Divine Soul Emerges from Glacial Waters

[•]

Rearview reductionism
34   is what it has been coined.

[••]

Both pelagic & benthic activities
are known, but generally bottom feeders
reap inordinate benefits
over surface dwellers.

35

[•••]

36   What mental maps
do you maintain
from your own habitat?

[●●●●]

More is seen on the ebb tide
than the slack, has been said.
& this, of course, is driven
by god-given celestial bodies:
so sayeth the god-fearing, god-attending holy folk.

[⊙]

Drift during a full moon,
currents are stronger.

38

You must face them
to reap the benefits
of being pressed
back into the fastest
moving slipstream.

[•••] *blood* confidante

Another Mysterious Blood Cult

Some say the Smiths emerged
from an active volcano.

Others say
those divine beings

were the first Smiths
who forged the volcano themselves

from their very own metal bones
in the primal waters,

42   & anointed
the copperwood trees

& their roots, & metastasized
across the as-yet-unknown world,

founding the first cities
blooming hot in iron ore.

Fabulously Exotic Flowers

All the hummingbirds
hover here

for a few seconds
listening to seeds

43

murmur in a bold
bristling heart.

Linear B-2 translation from a fresco in a tavern in Magenticum

A root form.
A form of root.
A gnostic rooting-out.

Algae. Fungi. Protozoa:
a unit of cosmic
reproduction

44

as the opposite
of that which divides
infinity

(from herself).

Linear B-2 translation from a leather tag on a vase containing dried magick mycelia in Nova Sepharia

Time Cubed

A short-
cut cut-
ting his-
tory sh-
ort; but,
who ow-
ns our vis-
ions of a fu-
ture, &,
who is
miss-
ing
?

A short-cut cut-ting his-tory sh-ort; but, who ow-ns our vis-ions of a fu-ture, &, who is miss-ing ?

? ? ? ing miss- who is ns our vis- ture, &, ions of a fu- ort; but, who ow- tory sh- ting his- cut cut- A short-

ing
miss-
who is
ture, &,
ions of a fu-
ns our vis-
who ow-
ort; but,
tory sh-
ting his-
cut cut-
A short-

[•]

Emanation

A vibrant
string from
the spiral
of creation.

[••]

Illumination

A burst
of light
ensnared
in a wound
of night.

47

[•••]

Insemination

In com-
passion,
a god
crawls
out of
the empt-
iness.

[••••]

Inebriation

Walking
the dark
& lonely
corridors
like the first
ghosts.

49

[☉]

Instigation

Sired into
the cosmos
by a giant bat
once named
Esmeralda.

50

[🜨 •]

Elevation

Beyond ours
is another
who holds us
our place for
all eternity.

[⊙••]

Libation

More than
this is not
known——&,
what is, is
also
barely
known.

Fragments of a City Called ⊘ in Linear B-2

*C7330-7Ae: scroll fragment in pottery urn, human remains,
snake-woman image*

The young ones scamper
across rectangular passages of time.

The older search
for just the right square.

The even-older hold still
on their quadratic root.

Meanwhile, the ancients plan
the next best move.

53

C947-9H: broken wax seal, five fragments

[•]

An escape from
the corporeal,
a facile lurch
into the beyond—

54

[••]

As if plunging
through one's own
many reflections—

[•••]

& then descending
into a long narrow
funnel that carries
you out—

[••••]

into the other—

[☉]

more illum-
inated side—

58

C1039-54e: two fragments wrapped around a human tibia

[•]

Dearest Marcellino,

Sending you our heartfelt sour grapes. The vinegary wine you poured me is rather empty. Still, may the Will of the One live within you both as human & specter […]

I hate to be so practical, but […] I think you took me for a sucker on that last deal […] with the three lame Dandelion ewes. They were cheap, since they could barely totter, but still produced the most voluptuous ewe's milk: creamy, frothy, the substance of clouds, you'd said.

59

Actually, their milks squirted out rancid & stinking of ghastly demonic fringe elements. The rumbles could be heard all the way to the Fire Temple. The aunties complained their cheesecakes were turning out lumpy & soggy. Many cities have subsisted in swampland, but this is ridiculous! they said.

I cleverly explained it was all in the reptile eggs they were using——& the elbow motion […]

Yours anxiously,

Muritanio

[••]

Dearest Muritanio,

As you will know by now: I am not to be trusted.

Still, I am not without my advantages.

Actually these were three of my favorite ewes.

May I suggest that the milk in question be applied in the manufacturing of a soft-cured curdled cheese that pairs well with hard-boiled March rodents & black olives. I am sure this will appeal to the elaborate tastes of your own infamous City of Ø.

Please accept this gift of curds & whey as a token of mutual understanding.

Blessings to your wife & barnyard fowl.

May the Will of the One, & so on & so forth [...]

Marcellino (dictated but not proofread)

C1039-55e: scroll wrapped around a bear's shinbone

A Heightened Stony Awareness

& the years narrowed stealthily,
& it was ascertained that the populace
required an entertainment

in lieu of, or, perhaps in addition to the Games:
in those early years, as Culture proliferated,
attention spans waned

(attention was paved with all manner
of troves), & *Her Immaculate Book of Slag*
had been passed down centuries ago

from the first Smiths of Iron,
they who appeared in the eye of the coal,
all-consumed with heated passion:

after all, it was the Great Heat
that formed us all in the center of our sun—
first as a liquid, then a vapor,

gaseous for an instant,
then, finally, we coagulated
into a solid mass, a bouncing ball.

CI039-55e: four-word inscription on the fossilized eye of a praying mantis

Eye
of
a
beholder

Religion?

Religion can be anything
you need it to be, was said.
It can justify existence or

be justified into existence, was said.
It can be a titan or a bodhisattva
or even a damaged demigod, was said.

It might be the mud
you trail in on your shoe, was said.
Others welcomed religion, embraced it

like the sure thing it was, wrote songs
& psalms & chants & arias
praising the glory of their object of adoration.

Still others believed they were above it,
claiming it fogged the mind & hemmed one in.
Eventually, at a legendary confluence of philosophers,

polemicists & part-time politicians, it was decided
that there needed to be a unifying theory
that would satisfy all the practical citizenry:

64 Make it mysterious, was said.
Make it archaic, was said.
Make it infinite, was said.

STRATUM B:

a house of mirth

Anonymous Inscription on the Stele of Marcus Aesophagus

Think   not
who   he
said   he
was   but
who he
mi ght
ha ve
been

67

[•]

68

Every family in the province wished to earn enough to own both a raven & a serpent.

Few succeeded in this endeavor.

[••]

Some had either one or the other, which, according to *Her Immaculate Book of Slag*, might lead to all manner of imbalances concerning & within the family structure.

70

& then there were those who traveled to all corners of the globe sealing deals in commodities & sacred trade routes. Some of these who lived on the much coveted Ossetian coastline had both—& some, in the highest echelon even owned a copperwood tree that grew in a central holy yard in their holy homes where both the holy raven & the holy serpent dwelled.

[●●●●]

These holy creatures, of course, were just symbols of fire, of the lust that drove us mechanically, chemically, psychoemotionally.

& thus enflamed, we forged the divide between the provincial & the psychoemotional cosmopolitan.

[⊙]

72

& then a day appeared, coming forth in a stringent morning, laced with caffeine & barbiturates & carbohydrates.

[☉•]

It turned into stringent night.

Fleas Fleas Fleas

The drought plagued us seven late summers:
what water & corn there was, we shared
among the Common Populace.

As it got colder we lost our leaves,
& then, a little later, we lost our color.
Overhead the skies remained shifting, dark,

rainless clouds for weeks & weeks & weeks,
until finally, on one mild mid-winter day there was a break,
& a single burst of sunlight shone through

74   & illuminated a single withered stalk on the dusty plain.
An ant was there carefully sawing it in two.
A cricket hopped wildly, jerked, then died.

Sun? said some. What we need is water.
& downpour it did, but not water, fleas. Fleas like rain.
But it is not yet the end! roared the Sages raising their shiny ironwork.

But it is! roared the Common Populace waving their dirty weapons.
& the Great Enchanter mounted the serpentine stairs
& laid their hands palm-down on a heaving human chest

& cut out the heart, & ate of that still beating flesh,
until those bloods had seeped into the cracks & crevices
of the holy Fire Temple & finally reached the divine.

An Industry Titan, Then

[•]

A successor? he said, looking you squarely
through his atomically-charged industrial eye.

None could be found, he said
scrolling through his old dog-eared ledgers.

But wait! Here was one: a woman
hewn of chalk & lime with a beveled fossilized nature

(we all know the sharp curve
is the preferred aesthetic of the industrialists—

& if derived from the cold acetone that color-coded itself,
anything could be surmised).

75

[••]

& so he contemplated how many fingers
she might have on one hand,

& he commissioned a cryptoduplicate
with her own cryptofingers to pluck the flowers

in the gardens of his own *Petit Château* on Lac LeValoussie,
& he dressed her in a straw boater & a white linen suit,

(& throughout the summer had her provide passage
to wayward tourists & a smattering of paparazzi,

for he knew how she would answer when asked:

Anything could be surmised, she would have said).

Eight Three-Line Line-Worker Digs

[•]

Who toils for the nation
to heat the oil to power our starlets
for a billion years?

[●●]

Aren't the hot coals
in the oven intent
on making more **bread**?

[•••]

Don't we have a **billion** years
of fossils to burn up
in less than a **million**?

[••••]

Aren't iron & coal twins
forged from the same
singed tree of life?

[⊙]

Is not that rascal raven
the color of coal &
oil & iron & bilious coke?

81

[⊙•]

Doesn't **one** seam
seem more
than **an other**?

[⊙••]

In the universe
isn't there more
dark than light?

83

[⊙•••]

Isn't there a **diamond**
to be found
in every other seam?

84

The Reinvention of Numbers

How do you count
a billion years?

Do you begin
at year naught?

Or do you begin
at year naught plus one?

Tiny Recipe for Intellectual Dumplings

We'll
talk

stuffing
first,

then bite;

later,
chew, chew, chew.

The Shape of a Bite

Some have teeth sharp as knives,
others the soft yet firm pull

of the proboscises; some tear
& twist to release tissue

from tendon & bone, others
like the weeping sparrow, wear their food

in woeful feathers. The Smiths say
there was an era when the only thing edible

far & wide was radiation & sunlight;
in those days the world thrived,

& the shape of a bite did not make you
into the deadliest weapon.

The Flying Netherlandian Cling Film Factory

[•]

How it was that the Flying Netherlandian became a symbol of our sticky plastic film? or, that, indeed, all manner of unfinished meals might be sealed in, or, by the fate of a Netherwoman who flew & blew?

Linear B-2e translation of fragments from journal entries discovered at the bottom of a beeswax candleholder in Magenticum

[••]

An inside joke suggested all manner of holy Netherlandish milk products must be spared those heated bacilli pirates, but also would be subject to the sacred laws of the high seas.

[•••]

&, many years later, after the Long Horde had laid down their shields, one of those hairy faux Flyssons, a fellow by the name of Martha, I believe, dared promise the stockholders excessive returns (something to do with the discovery of an as-yet untapped oil reserve in the Sepherian highlands where the Holy Ravens were known to cohabit).

[••••]

&, given that we ourselves resided in a former
tropical paradise, the stock went soaring wildly into
all our virtual stratospheres.

[⊙]

Later, X or Y or Z generations disapproved of the entire silky-sticky-clingy-slinkiness & tossed it all out & turned to a slinky-crinkly-waxy paper.

[⊙•]

& thus the Flying Netherlandian was reborn as a wax paper factory—which, according to certain risk-averse investors was:

[⊙••]

the ideal medium to bundle up fresh-farmed fish & soggy French fries, & was perfectly soluble in all manner of lipids & liquids.

At least, thus read the official approval seal from the Iron Pier Society.

The Sun Who Emerged from the Womb of Night

Our Sacred Enigmatic Bubble

Doesn't burst.

Doesn't even

crack a hair. She re-

mains resolute, vacuum-

sealed within thickening cell

walls, emblematic, self-con-

tained, emboldened with

a peculiar sense of

cellular purpose.

Once in a Cosmos

Funny though
how things come a-
part quite the same way
they puzzle back together:
once we called her our
Big Burst, but now
reticently refer
to her as our
Grand Rebound.

& Still There Were Other Sparks

In the Original Fires,
through augury & divination
the Founding Smiths discovered

we were divinely ignited as the heavens
parted——&, like a spark to a pyre,
the essence of our primeval selves

seeded a barren, empty earth;
but in that rocky prehistoric era, the Smiths say,
volcanoes brewed & bubbled & sluiced——

98

& eventually half the world was smoking, singed
& melting; & they also say, we walked
the white-hot lines with bare feet long before

she cooled; &, according to the Smiths,
from the ashes emerged a bird
whose fiery plumage lit up the atmospheres,

bestirring clouds & snows & incandescence;
& across the planet this bird was known
by many names from phoenix to griffin

to the Furaribi, or perhaps the twelve-winged
Chalkydri, who apparently dwells near the surface of the sun;
but we, we called her our Dear Mother Oil:

the Will of the One searing through the blood of earth—
& later, to meet more popular demand,
the Smiths invented other myths

with rocketships & aeroplanes & cryptotwits;
& with these too, we metaphorically charged
& reentered the world again—

but, also once again, in retaliation,
the universe expanded
(every so often she has to inhale);

& for us too, eventually, it was not enough:
that primal urge to seed goes beyond,
deep into the Great Unknown, &,

beyond space & time & faith, beyond
eternity, into a mirror of alternative realities,
until, eventually we just fizzle out.

A Fragment of a Hotel Upon a Hill at the End of the World

She waves from a wrought-iron balcony,
smiling with her sparkling wine.

The rest of us are
below beachcombing.

We squeeze into our wetsuits
& weed out lost continents.

So, Time is the Ignition

& Space her messy lover.

The Golden Fruits of the Ø Tree

Some will tell you
it has to do
with the versatility

of their uses. How
the stones might
plug up an ear; or, if,

after death, inserted
into an opened nostril,
invariably prevent the brain

102   from seeping out
into the sands of time;
others might decree

their grease among the most ancient
of ancient greases—
& therefore, of a broader vision:

squeezed from trees who breathed
their own city laurels, yelled
down country lanes

luxuriating radiance
from century to century,
now delivered their most

radiating succulence:
early societies gently bathed in it,
oiled their feet & hair with it—

yet also, when infused with lemon
& garlic & chives, dipped their bread
& gently ate of it.

A **Dark** Bird Speaks **Cold** Truths

Where are you?
Are you some **where**
where you are?
Or, are you some **where**
where you are
some **where** else?

A Cosmogony

A pale moon
sticks out

her tongue
at the center

of a sun;
a black hole

spinning in
the middle

of a galaxy
once harkening

to Sagittarius A,
in conster-

nation,
whorls in

her own fiery
constell-

ations;
meanwhile,

the universe too
swells into

her own
limitless …

… ness;
& back & forth

on Earth
the earthworms

ask an awk-
ward question:

How does
consciousness
expand so easily
in the dirt?

STRATUM C:

after the grand rebound

A Miso Soup Hangs Her Heavy Head

A comfort passed gently on.

A Small Continent Unveils Her Flat Surfaces
& Slinks Quietly into a Dark Corner

When all the dust has settled in her lustrous stuffing of costumed centuries: dead keratin & bone, cracked idolatries, fantastical mythologies, faked ideologies of a creator, prophet or sage, carpenter, shepherd, or fisherman; of the incumbent & the upstart, each shedding skins, yet honing in on a vigorous stake-holding:

Waste not, want not, was once said.

Use & reuse. (Reduce, reuse, recycle.)

Every little particle can be accrued into an island, even as she shifts across spacetime: the Smiths tell us nothing has been left behind, merely transposed, transformed, reimagined, reengineered, repurposed—

Does each century find a use for another of these as-yet-undiscovered elemental building blocks of life, as if they […] as if they might never run out?

(As if they might never run out, was once also said.)

A Cosmic Oxymoron

& when
  finally we
    can drift
      mindfully
        in endless
          space, will
            we settle
          down on
            another
        planet &
      just let
    our junk
  sink in?

Isle of the Dead

A holiday getaway
only accessible by light.

The Mayfly Codex

A smart **machine** will first consider
which is more worth its while:
to **perform** the given task, or, instead,
to figure some way out if it.

—Stanislaw Lem

The Codas

More Truths Dancing into the Hereafter

The All-Unseeing Eye Moves behind the Curtain

Mechanical Rats Crystalizing

Fatal Wounds Liberated through Hearing

The Interrogatory Reborn

A Common Stew

Mysterious Blue Eggs

After a Sad Trickle of Water the Ego Enters the Id

With Broad Heart & Short Memory

We danced through our magic garden,
planted as we pranced, seeded,
pollinated & then ran ahead fertilizing.

The Sun shone her illuminable rays.
The Rain wiled us in her willful ways.
From time to time we were guarded.

We devoted ourselves to the Will of the One.
In this way, we fashioned ourselves
a seat at the Custodians' table.

121

We never once contemplated our actions
would have consequences beyond the Will:
yet, sometimes there is a dichotomy

that simply can't be untangled no matter
how many IQ points have been assimilated,
as the Great Leader once said:

A specialist knows when to stop specializing:
in other words, it's not about the background noise,
but a single note that rings true.

The **All-Unseeing** Eye Moves behind the Curtain

We won't **observe** you, it was said.
Just you go on about your business, was said.
& so we watered our magic garden

in the **knowledge** that we were unseen.
Of course, that year, water was scarce,
the lakes & rivers & creeks bare & dry,

fish & beaver skeletons adorned the shores
in their ivory pleas; still the mayfly soared gracefully
above the bramble, prickly pears & rose thorns.

A glistening film clung on to the tree bark,
& the toadstools oozed & huffed & wheezed;
a solitary beaver attempted to build a bluff

upon a lonesome hill, where a few drops of dew
clung on to withered fronds of bamboo
still towering above the flaring rust of dawn.

124

Where there's the Will there's a rain, is said.
Anything you can imagine has happened, is said.
Today, on the other hand, is simply another day.

Mechanical Rats Crystalizing

When it all ran dry, we realized
water had to be reassigned by the Will of the One.
As such, we finally came to the conclusion

the only solution was to insert the mechanical rats.
Technology is a glass marvel, after all, it was said.
The man with the glass eye unsees you from here too, was said.

Glass, of course, was first annealed in a crafty desert.
The Phoenicians & their forebears had once spread the word:
from Cartagena to Corinth all & everyone crystalized.

The succulents gave themselves away, though.
The sand vipers slithered into their own solitude.
The mechanical rats became denizens of a desert nation.

They needed no water to survive, was said.
They felt no sentient emotion, was said.
They didn't breed like rabbits, was said.

& thus the rats became our new Custodians.
They cleaned every surface until it shone like silver, &
with surgical precision, gleefully ate everything above the dirt.

Fatal Wounds Liberated through Hearing

We dry-heaved, we coughed up soot.
We injected serums, infusions, root solutions.
In a manner of speaking, we found religion again.

The brass toilet seat upended seemed like a halo.
The paper roll, a prayer wheel often spun counterclockwise.
Words incanted like a psalm for the dearly departed.

We strayed our days in cafés along the boardwalk.
We painted towers & trestles & tetrahedrons.
We found light in the staccato & the pulse of the hot city.

We loved the night. We receded into the corners of our minds.
We reunited with fallen famers, dust-bowlers, dark-matter denouncers.
We endured incontinence, premature ejaculation, excision, tattoos.

We needed nothing to survive, was said.
What about the nomenclature? was asked.
We don't breed like rabbits, was said.

128

We lived in the here-&-now, strove through
the theretofore, painted pictures like silver,
swirled, misted up, then rose back to the surface.

The Interrogatory Reborn

Whereas beneath the surface was what mattered....
Whereby the man with the glass eye unsees you from here too, is said.
Whereas the tidal forces aid in that predilection for pride.

There too, Mercury pushes his point with a winged helmet
cast in the forges of planetoids, in the foundries of solar systems:
Here too, a human is a marvel too splendid to behold;

but beyond the cast-iron face, beyond the funereal casket,
the drink-until-you-still, the wise man raises his elbow
& forces those fungal spores to rise into the heliosphere.

How a tidal force may be a station of happiness, or a slug,
devoid of all friction, how a mercurial body thrusts their point
into all that breathes in this heady carbon dioxide.

Ethereal is what we called it, once upon the Blue Divide.
Sulfurial is what we wished it, once upon the Cardboard Wall.
& still, the mystery that we call the Great Unknown

has been spilled, foamy & sanctified by the One
in the word of the Common Spirit, that each & all shall devour
the warm words served up with pork dumplings & cabbage stew.

A **Common** Stew

& here too the gaze that caught so much:
the contemporaries & their minute objects:
the polished-off antiquities brought into **mainstream** view:

of the waffle or the snuffle we've come to suffer too:
or so said Mother about her waifs; Father
was far too busy dredging his own liquid grave.

We all know those stories full of disgrace
& disgust, whereby history tumbles about your ears:
memory is selective, **elective**, fills in cracks & **tears**.

Either way, the tide will carry you if you wish it or not:
the trolling waves ride up the last rocky outcrops:
the seabirds still hover here, grabbing & pulling & plucking,

seething in their own dewy, frothy brew—at least here
the world seems to appear for a second or two:
& still the mystery calls us back into the Great Unknown.

132

We broiled & basted for hours among the shitting pigeons & bats,
we sought out major viral afflictions, all for a historical panorama:
to watch that gorgeous flag raised up the ethereal flagpole.

Mysterious Blue Eggs

& when all the hens' eggs were devoured, folks descended
upon the crags & cliffs, clinging to mossy outcrops: little hardy fowl
clasping the substrata hoping for a drought to pass over.

Here they forged & fenced their intentions, housed
into the lateral view, squared away with their pretensions, usurped
& upended the all-held-belief, until, later, it became a life or a brief

hard to argue with: so was said, or so sometime once said:
Where there's the Will, there's the One, was once said.
Fork in hand: Eat not to be eaten, was also widely said.

Sharp protruding objects should be avoided, was clearly said.
Dead lead need not be burdened, was once said.
Lift yourself above the masses & puff out your chest, was said;

but above all, bring out those **beautiful** mysterious blue eggs.
Meanwhile, we prayed to the dead & dying hoping
they would send us maps of the Great Unknown

to guide our way into the Aftersurface:
They failed, & we ran amok, ran astray, ran away, upended.
Until once again the **heavens** descended.

After a Sad Trickle of Water the Ego Enters the Id

Some said even mention of it was absolute heresy:
the Will of the One was not to be cross-examined.
Just as the language of the Ancients was not to be spoken

by an other than the scientist in their eureka moments
on the rim of a golden toilet bowl—or so the saying goes.
But then, what's said is truly never said, is also said.

Funny, how looking out into the distant valley
you might never recognize how many have disappeared
never to be seen again—least not here, on this side

of the Great Unknown where eternal enemies vie
for apex-predator status beneath the surface of cryptospace.
Doesn't biomimicry account for 97% of what we know? was once said.

Did we model ourselves upon the termites or the tigers? was asked.
Did we once worship them as we worshipped the One?
Even the scientists struggled to see deep into the Great Unknown.

136

But the Great Unknown glanced back, unrelentingly, until,
one fine day, as the sun rose & feral creatures settled in their nests,
once again, the heavens ascended, or so it has been said.

She stripped the bark & munched the soft-fleshy under-bough,
right between the lines of storm years, when the mayflies—
every hundred years or so, seek out the most prolific pastures.

In these years they rise high into the lower thermals,
their thin-skinned wings at risk of tearing even in a minor gale:
But just who measures wind or love, my little mercies?

So says the unwitting Will of the One turning their Common Pages—
& yet they walked through the quick-shooting eucalyptus trees
looking for a mate to unburden their conscience—at least, so was said

by the scientists, crossing their loose fingers—& hoping
we might crossbreed two gods into one, said one.
Another said, Even though her acorns may sleep in the shade,

a tree will always seek out the sun. Somewhere a voice
quietly nattering was pulling little levers in their cortex,
then said quietly: Isn't an acorn a tree in the making?

&, unseen, the Great Unknown cast their sharp eyes upon
an illegible script, something transcribed over a millennium ago,
once called the Vast Memory, now simply named the Reward.

To live, in other words,
is to possess a **future**
which will become
your **present**.

—Stanislaw Lem

Eons Later

There should be
a cooling shade,
a first form once said

amongst the orange groves
near the river by the sea;
a second cooed: Remember

what they said? They said:
Flush them out! & we floated
through the sewers &

into a deep tidal swell.
A third form, unaware of
the words dribbling down

their protruding chin, said:
Once, an intrepid form
of fortitude found a flame.

A Most Beguiling Iron Age Fantasy

& fire was discovered in the eye of the coal.
& life was discovered in the eye of the fire.

&, in life, all things tended toward the hearth,
toward the music & the lyre, the songs & chants

of forms aspiring to thrive within, & the eye that looked out
from beneath the eye, & the eye from within the eye

where there are plains & oceans unknown—but,
as you surely know, we were taught that everything that exists

can only exist because it exists somewhere else, even in absentia.
No less unnerved, we still convinced ourselves little

can be grown from nothing at all—& yet, intervention
from the other side occurred: by that the citizens referred

to the Great Unknown: or, as a great philosopher
haphazardly once declared: Humanity must remain

eternally aroused: for how otherwise could a culture flourish
beyond the eternally piling mountains of ash & fire & time.

A Metal Liturgy

    & so, in a rapture, we wrote a song to praise the metals in the universe; & how, in tender union with fire, the beating heart of Mother Earth poured us across her milky surfaces.

    & seizing the flame someone planted a seed in the last corner of the world, hidden in a steel trapezoid forged in the Mountains of Mercy by the most ancient of Smiths. They were once aptly named, but now […].

    Still, the last Ice Age endures.

    & we sing on.

& how did the Smith know how to forge, or the forger know how to smith? Such were the questions represented at the first Annual Convention of the Grand Emporium (notwithstanding the Poor Standard Corporation, a fabricator of crypto-currencies, long since abandoned by the Abundances).

& just how would a man dress without his medals & buttons & tassels & tinsels & tongs?

The going joke that convention was: How would you fancy walking about in your musty, flea-infested sheepskins? Or could you really imagine shoes without their steel toecaps? It was most laughable. & there were many other such airy & inflated conflagrations that first convention.

144

Sinjay ordered the plates of the caskets fastened with security rivets & bolts made of a very peculiar shiny alloy; the Smiths, on the other hand, felt they had always paid the price.

The Flyssons stepped in & in their unilateral-eco-commerce way both seeded & started a movement:
a movement which became what we now call

the End Movement ...

A Strange Deluge

There was no forewarning
when the waters rose.

Something exotic
emerged from the sea

& overtook the last pinnacles
of mud & rock.

We wondered why the sun & moon had become
so bored with each other.

Once, the Smiths called upon Them:
& from beneath the waters, they slithered forth

onto the stones & the sand,
& learned to worship the sun

as the Enchanted Peoples
of the Republic of Ø.

Seizing the Mantle of Liberty

Stones are easily thrown, is said.

Atonement, on the other hand,
is as hard won as a brick of gold.

To guide the perplexed home,
cast a beacon of light, was once widely
proclaimed early Sunday mornings.

.

Tiny Poem on Telekinesis

Eighty-six billion
neurons gave us
the power
to transform
the weight
of the world.

148

Linear B-2 fragment from a fresco in a bordello in Ossetia

Every Second Ending in Trottelheim

Begins like

this:

STRATUM D:

a common wheel, a common prayer

A Common Wheel

With which to drive an ox.
With which to feed
a practical constituency:

With which to wind, rewind,
& cut a thread, divide ahead
with practical cellular purpose:

With which to mechanize a tractor;
or, in the memory of a civilization or two,
find a common lottery & seal a practical vote:

As once, upon a field of dead soldiers,
raising his sword, a General said:

Once, upon a bright new snow.

Fragments of a City Called ⦰ in Linear B-2a

F743-1A: Seven fragments found at the bottom of a broken vase

A Trip to the Moon

[…] early in our history, people believed
there lived another race of giants like us […]

[…] on the Moon […]

154

[…] you could tell by their waterworks
they were an impressive group of individuals
who, much like us must follow the Will of the One;
& so, at the earliest opportunity, when Mother Oil
& Father Fire entwined […]

[…] we sent a rocketship to the moon. & what we discovered
exceeded human dimensions.

We were no longer alone in the universe.

We were just perhaps not the smallest ones.

F947-13Y: gold-plated shell of an unknown species of millipede
(presumed talisman)

For Ludmilla:

Don't let these skinny
little legs fool you.

I travel further to-
ward you every day

F2135-2Ae: leather vellum sealed with lead & stamp marked
◉◉◉

Zero Oh Zero

> *Zero:*

Either way, each of these represent nothing more
than an empty exasperation—a sigh at most.

> *Oh:*

Still, out of the nothingness of the furthest cosmos
emerged something that was a little more than zero.

> *Zero:*

Oh, so Oh you're saying I am less than zero?
How can nothing be the beginning of something?

> *Oh:*

Shh, a mellow wind stirs the snow in the stars now.

F78929B: wax seal on cork in an amphora, serpent image

Bronze   Her snake eyes
betray nothing.

Copper   His bilious eyes
betray everything.

Iron   Their starry eyes
betray the moon.

Titanium   Eye to eye, gather here
& betray us one & all.

Esoterium   Turn your eyes inward,
betray no one, live free!

Solistorium   Raise your eyes, Darling,
& stare into the center of the sun.

Conspictium   Don't eye me,
I've been blindsided.

G8893A: golden ring with jadeite insert

Three active compound verbs
upon a copperwood tree:

Upward-peeling!
Outward-calling!
All-unseeing!

The Melanchordist

Somehow he heard the afternote,
but was unable to contradict it.

How often had these overtones been used
to sway urges & re-urges—waves & waves

of tonal anomalies in the lower registers,
layers of meaning hinted at, but never confirmed,

spectral mists rising & swirling—& yet somehow
the afternote […]

The **Enchanted** Codex
of the Peoples
of Ø

The Lost City of Ooze

[•]

Seventeen Leagues Northwest into the jungle & deep into the interior, follow the scurrying path of the speckled bull lizard until you reach the Quicksilver Falls where the quiverfish leap the currents, then hop, skip & jump carefully along the ancient riverbed. You will reach an overgrown & decimated sign that reads:

"These deadly shores
are home to the sand serpent …"

signed & sealed *Holisiticiifcus* ••

[••]

These creatures have long been considered extinct.

"[…] & the venomous dross beetle […]"

[•••]

Hasn't been around since the last quarter century.

It goes on to say:

"(when it turns sheeny & oily, you know you are close):"

"[…] she will arise from the foliage like a winged serpent
above & beyond the hills spreading
her long tentacles […]"

[••••]

The location of the lost city remains desperately unknown.

Cryptofingers

Envied by industry titans
& their well-heeled magnates & moguls,
sages, astronomers, & smiths;
it was said, those with cryptofingers
could peel back layers in a flick
or a snap or a whip, & could count
in multiples of seven point five to half a dozen or more;
in the former days, these folk were said
to be enchanted by the iron & her blessed ore;
still others were distrustful
& took to wearing dark leathers
in protest, claiming the cryptofingers
had a devious plan to conquer
the known world; several great leaders
& industry titans intervened,
promising great abundance to all
in the form of further luxuries
to soothe sinking souls;
in the end, of course,
once again, a common
sense & a practical self
prevailed & the cryptofingers
were left to their many useful devices
& necessary contrivances.

A Silent Purge

The Flyssons, in their enviable cryptofingers,
ensnared the common populace in a rapture
of hot commodities & semi-toxic substances
that flared up the mind of the lesser-understood:

There was a word for it: Moonpeoples!
Moonpeoples had spread their cryptofingers!
What mattered, they said was that these things
made of a matter were what truly mattered.

168   Mostly, we nodded in ascent as they ascended,
& from their ascent, under the mechanical eye
of the industry skins, they looked down
& pointed out our many flaws & cockups,

reminding us that value exists only in expansive growth,
& that any advantage conferred by Mother Oil
or, in this case, the Moonpeoples, who swore
by the Old Iron Ore & all its exquisite entrails clasped within,

that they were here on Earth to spread wisdom
& union & harmony & a deep ancient love that arose
from the farthest reaches of the nearly infinite.

We didn't really believe them.

Various Earlier Forms

[•]

Suspicious Aliens Appear on Cuthbert's Sulfur Plains

Lizards in mammalian form,
breathing anorexic foam,
emerge from a bluish ovum;

170   Titus startles in the warmed water,
Julietta rises from her soft skins,
watches bubbles rising-swirling,

until everything cools down;
then suddenly, a gorgeous
candelabra reemerges & reoccurs.

[••]

Dead Kestrels Hint at the Downfall of a Civilization

These were days that other young lady
proclaiming the end of days in her bright blue pajamas
suggested each & every moment would be tallied out

in the Great Uncertain——&, in life, who too could believe
those tall tales of aliens who finger-picked whose farm
might plant their diametrically opposed offspring—

they came from our own Moon through the clouds, after all—
though different in their reflections, were just like us, shining on.
To reflect is to cast out a star, our Great Leader once said gently.

[•••]

Morphogenesis

From the under-
wings

of a temple,

the undetermined eye

of a flagging tower

          stares off
into the distance:

but, the Will of the One
is clearly all laid out …

                    … incidentally.

The First Spores

[•]

Beware the love of
well-informed beauty—

the luxuriant qualities
of fatty mare's milk,

the lavender & soap
you soothe yourself in—

without which you wouldn't
be caught dead or alive.

173

[••]

At the lectern,
a Sage leans

a hard forward
into the attentive

174   & intelligent
gathering

who will soon
begin to swoon.

A Fifth Dimension

U M
A M
M i

Linear B-2 fragment from a fresco in a tavern in Magenticum

Naming Absent Gods

The land was filled
with the fertility of the Prolific One, yet
we knew we had done something wrong.

Had we planted the wrong seed?
Seeded the wrong plant?
All the mushrooms in the world, said someone,

what are all their names again?
The Will is a self-defining thing, it grows
within you—it's the core of your nervous system.

176

A scientist intervened, & said we got it all wrong.
Henceforth each & every god
had to have a name.

The All-Unseeing Eye Moves further
behind the Derailed Curtain

[•]

We won't observe you, it was said: we observe other things,
like smooth fabrics quivering in the opulent breeze; little
pinecones scattering haphazardly at our whitehot feet, one
said; only, it rang untrue—at least this was what circulated in
our bloodwork, through tunnels & funnels & pipework stoking
fumes in the canteens & on park benches—

177

& yet, each & every Moonday morning as the cockerel crowed & the sun could barely be made out through the charred cumulus, most of us set out to **toil** among the fields or up into the icy mountains;

but some of us entered the very caverns of our bubbling Mother Oil, where we scooped & canned & we barreled on—

[•••]

Until eventually Father Fire flowed forth—

[••••]

& a million times we were burning the torches & bonfires; a million times more we found fortune in the Five Flaming Fates who were said to cleanse the earth of all her filthy impurities.

[⊙]

But it was only when the First Fires had turned to **ash**—

[⊙•]

that Dirt found her first form.

182

A Small Sense of Cooling Proportion

In the longhand & cooling perspective of myth, a spatula rings out in little wooden echoes, but returns cunningly to her moment of complete tree-silence.

Stirring, we leap into each other's eyes & whisper our fiery intentions.
It all adds up.

& we count the stars, multiply domains respectfully, divide the shoals & oceans; & happily, the seabirds go on singing & plucking strings.

Some great leader once said: Inflation is the heady incline of cost over time.

Evolution cunningly centers herself, happy & deep in the recesses of a dominant genome.

Even though I am myself recessive, I believe in that, someone said.

To eat is to be young & vibrant; to starve is to seek out the Great Unknown.

But I ask you, honestly: What can beat the quivering of a lone molecule of oil?

EPISTRATUM:

a prophet is born
somewhere else
every other day

More Paranormal Social Schedules

When antipodal & bipedal,
the modal proportions belie

their true nature—for isn't
everything naturally destined for the sea?

High Appeals Court

How to
disprove any-

one is as
they appear?

Linear B-2e graffiti in public toilet in Trottelheim

A Post-Metaphysical Sting

Surfaces again,
but only in twilight,

or betwixt the flight
of a star-billed few.

For even in uneven
Showbiz years,

there is a brief pause …
& in the cold cold morning

when concrete sets
on the highrise, we renounce

the resplendent few
with their descending views,

& their broad-brimmed-
broad-handed-cigar-loaded-

side-glances into
the original embers.

First things first: Who, after all,
wants to remain tied up

190

in a loop of their own
muscle memory?

The All-Unseeing Eye Finally Sees

& what she saw was once written.

Fire of all things
is Judge & Ravisher.

—Heraclitus

But Fire is also Redeemer.

—She, The Prophet, She

On the Irønclad Origin & Design of the Species

An Address to the Iron Plier Society IPS®
on the Opening of the Five Strata in Situ

by Citizen-Smythe Jean-Paul Flysson-Sasson, iBBS, IPS®

Dearest Citizen-Smythes & Holy Grantors & Grantees:

[•] Context

To state the absolute & almost obnoxiously obvious—even from the mind of an Unbeliever—in the contorted context of what has been termed historical record, much of the narrative presented here hails from the mind of a visionary catcher of souls.

Despite all our modern pursuits & commonalities—the fiery eons that have throbbed & collapsed into layers of ash & slag & coal—we now know iron transforms wisdom into ideas, & then through her infinite alchemy transmits profound metaphysical knowledge.

She will remain firm & resolute until three thousand degrees Flysson; until she liquefies into our pyrotechnical Motherblood & courses across our timid centuries. Many precarious civilizations have been engulfed by her molten essences never to be heard of again; some sages have said it was a heavenly requirement that we were rekindled & resparked several times. Our sly, adaptable genes were bumping into each other & steadily firing their own sparks: slowly learning, acquiring, trading multimucosal squirtings of information, mis-, or even, dis-information.

Even disinformation can be revealing, the First Smith intoned at the flames of the First Fire.

The sun has not yet risen on the horizon, yet even now, in this far distant future, some semblance of our ur-progenitors' instinct still clings on: in myth, in art, in ritual, even in dastardly deed. Whiffs of these long-departed influences can still be sensationalized broadly, particularly at birthings, unions, & public burnings.

Can we divine the future by reaching into the past?

Almost as unfamiliar as those elusive words echoing from *The Enchanted Codex of the Peoples of Ø*: 'cryptofingers', the undecipherable 'cryptocurrencies', & that upper-quadrant leap to 'Moonpeoples'—they still resonate through our mantles & joints; they ring convincingly through our thickest skins. The concept of life beyond our stratosphere was conceived very early on, it seems—in the patterns of clouds, in the 'cryptopatterns' of the kittywakes crossing rising thermals, in the yellowing & tumbling leaves of autumn & the bright-sprouting lotus fungi.

Clearly many of these archaic concepts are nuanced, fine-tuned-&-finely-laced to the orders & powers of their eras (some of them perhaps mythological, some even clearly quite fictional): observances & analyses of systematic &/or reoccurring patterns in heavenly bodies; tidal shifts & weather patterns; earthquakes & sulfurous erupting mountain chains; in the flocking of starlings, or the steely swarming of firelocusts. Patterns repeating in rows, columns tightly packed in with the primordial, but evidently visible in hard, tangential, clanging matter; patterns repeating & repeating, with & without meaning.

As the First Smith once said: All meaning is in the eye of the ontological beholder—god, sage, smith, shepherd, or sorrel sheep.

Some of these earlier patterns are still discernable as omens. & even for the deeply skeptical, they have been proven to ignite the scientific mind—for does not the smoke of wisdom always cling on.

The renowned classical metaphysician Epifracsitus Furioso once asked if the value of a people was to be determined by how they handed down their own inherited knowledge. Given that the first known written language was largely divinatory in nature, we can only deduce that society is built on the fringes of metaphor, allegory, allusion, & parable.

How much, then, is literal & how much allegorical? & who decides what finds its way into the ontological record?

All archeologists are aware that systematic surveillance & an increase in fieldwork establish a geological context.

Does that which is not left behind determine the discerning mind that is divided to this very day?

& honestly, can you truly judge a people on their shoddy paperwork?

Others shout antipathy for crude, light-headed antecedents. After all these eons, foolish pride still rattles from rooftops. & most of us, admitting it or not, feel obliged—nay, spellbound—to eavesdrop on those kaleidoscopic conversations from before glowing coals & flint marks on mammoth tusk.

How much too, you ask, is imprinted in the fires of the genome?

& how much acquired, flame by flame, along the way?

The Iron Continuum of technological development is often surprisingly cell-altering. Time, as has been proven, is relative to the space where you currently occupy your own spacetime.

Following the linear narrative of supposedly sequential events is surely a mammalian approach: the sifting of coals & sands, the recurrent one-foot-in-front-of-another, the repetitious crashing of waves on the shore, the tick-tick-ticking of the crickets sawing through a summer's day—& the backward-pedaling too: all those copperwood trees & their hammocks; & on the edges, the wooly socks filling up with rain.

The Iron Continuum, however, we now know, is multilayered, multiparous, & continually evolving.

Although we had promised ourselves not to inject our own cultural & moral wont into these testaments, we cannot be sure we entirely succeeded in that endeavor.

("In context, given the human propensity to see objects & ideas through their own parochial worldview … The value of a given object is subject to its local needs," Ø-Laureate, Dr. Elias Flexious Flysson-Smythe.)

Human error was once called a divine fruit.

Naturally, we also cannot assume that creator of said lyric, inscription, epitaph or epigraph did not infuse some of their own fiery breath & wont into said statement(s); after all, much that has been written is propaganda, rhetoric, polemic, dogma, twisted iron. & much of it has been finely polished by the bards & their guadelopes.

Can we then illuminate the past so the future actually becomes clearer?

Seldom, if at all, has an artist been permitted the moral freedom they yearn for, or indeed earn for. Tastes, cultural morays & normalcies & shifts & fluxes of allegiances have to be pandered to. Flags & crests, plumage, jewelry, make-up & fancy hairdos help in this endeavor.

My mother, for example, always favored the high-heeled shoe & danced & tottered gingerly. My father, with his industrialist handlebar moustache, favored his Westerns & crosswords & chewing tobacco. Take it outside, Mother always said.

Many nights I spent with my old Fa (him deeply masticating his dried & pungent leaves, me gently sipping frothed whitleberry cordial through a flat straw) staring at the shooting stars, wondering which of the gods would bless our household the next Persimmon year.

One autumn night, he turned to me introspectively & asked which one I wanted (star or god, that is). With my crooked index finger, I pointed one out; he reached up with his hand & plucked it out of the sky & offered it to me as one might the last Ironblossom of the season.

I pinned her to my lapel for many years. & even though she only existed in my transcended self, she became the companion of my adolescence & led me erroneously to make what to me at that time seemed like life-changing decisions.

Are such strange cultural habits also true of flora & fauna?

During mating season, over the course of a nine-day week or thereabouts, the male ladderfish collects multicolored pebbles & erects a concentric nest to entice a potential mate with bling until he runs out of colored ones—as a result, many nests are left half-finished, & are taken over in a great display of masculine bluff the following season; in a bluster, too, the female kroonbeetle preens & polishes her sharp antlers on the bark of the dying copperwood tree to augment her position within the purview of her chosen galactic constellation (mostly Andronitus with her whispering tongs & serpentine body [mainstream enologists & animal psychologists are convinced of this]); the whittleberry bush grows in translucent clusters along the most noxious fields & is home to hundreds of ebullient rodent colonies.

&, in the furthest cornices of the Fire Temple where the sagemoss grows abundantly, single-celled creatures grow impatient, flash their membranes, & pair up.

Excepting in extremely arid conditions—the Dancing Deserts of Dulakang, beyond the Thundering Overland Pillars, the Fressian Rocksalt Plains—organisms of all six-creature kingdoms have long devoured our perishable & transportable communication materials, but particularly mealy worms, magbeetles & various forms of meta-mycelium.

Words were scribbled & sewn on the perishable: woven in fabrics; scratched on hand-beaten tin plates; scrawled on hard-won copperwood papers. All of these materials were adoringly absorbed into the Iron Continuum & have henceforth been recycled by our greatest smiths.

Yet visual art was also hewn & chiseled on stone: it makes impressions on walls & steles, lines heady colonnades, & amply decorates monuments & magnificent confinements. Movements & ghosts echo down the spectral halls of all that last infinitude of concreteness & succinctness.

There are those who say we may soon be able to extract this forgotten wisdom from the Golden Fruits themselves. Others say, we already have, several hundred times—though their coarse, wiry membranes—journeyed to the Outer & Inner Atmospheres.

Ask any smithing metaphysician & they will tell you all of humanity's knowledge resides deep in the spores of the Golden Fruits of ∅.

[••] Definition

Some of the terms & spellings used in this testament are simply well-considered approximations of the Proto-Ossetian scripts we discovered in this eye-widening excavation. Some linguists have cast a sliver of doubt over their broad & varied interpretations, but isn't that always the case with a translation or transliteration? & excuse me for my unorthodoxy, but isn't everything a vague approximation of something else?

What is a flame to another flame, after all, dear Citizens?

We will, of course, address these considerations in detail later—& for those of you who may be interested in the philological methodology & comparisons that we have on record at various institutions across the pivot of the planet—please consult the latest research papers from The Flysson-Smythe Institute of Metallurgical & Metaphysical Endeavors. Seventeen new papers have been presented to the prestigious journal, *Iron Alchemy*, in this last month alone.

Many of the most renowned metaphysicians, sages, smiths, alchemists have analyzed these sometimes crude, but always crucial testaments within our current scientific limits down to the last cell quivering. Among other things, we discovered that our ur-progenitors had quite different concepts of numbers & colors.

In the Proto-Ossetian scripts (decoded by the illustrious Citizen-Smythe Frederica Faustina-Flysson), there are hues totally unknown to our own visual receptors. These addition colors have been transliterated phoneme by phoneme to: Ulembric, Sulfic, & the equally electrifying Electurion.

As far as numbers are concerned, according to our current methods of calculation, they just don't add up. For starters, it appears that our ancestors counted not in units of six or twelve, but for some as yet unknown reason, performed their calculations with variable units of seventeen & a half, & nine point seven, which in many cases is rounded up another third half of ten.

Our philological researchers have been entirely vexed that an earlier civilization—which we have supposedly hailed from—had an entirely alternative concept to the coloring of our ever-blooming world. Further scholarly analysis & review will be required in order to ascertain whether we will ever be able to reproduce these unknown visions faithfully.

Apologies to amassing later generations of metaphysicians, sages, & scientists; we have surely missed many finite nuances: we can only see as deep inside as our microscopes & their convex lenses allow. Of course, strata are catalogued according to their relative depths in the geological record (which in & of itself has its stony constraints), & are assimilated into the linear narrative in the successive manner in which they appeared while digging downward toward the molten heart of our pyrotechnical Motherblood.

(In our geological record, layers settle sequentially on top of each other. Is this the story of progress?)

We are now reducing our search for an original seed down to a common human genome that flourished across the planet in waves of hunter-gatherers up into the Plains, into the flooded Underlands, across the vast Himerian Wastelands.

The archeological record is slim, but ponderous.

Few have traveled beyond the last lighthouse overlooking the reef of Winsome Snails; &, some of you will know that the even-fewer-who-returned never quite possessed their own souls again. There are many theories—lunacy has been well attended over the Lunar Eons. Some involve the Divine Serpent Woman, others our holy twinned ravens—or perhaps it was the First Smith's discovery of the fire that burned in the heart of the first volcano.

Her Immaculate Book of Slag tells us:

Even as the cold moon looks on in apathy, our pyrotechnical Motherblood yearns to return into the cradling flames of her own Mother Sun.

Since the Long Common Era, we now appreciate this not as a literal truth, but as an allegory & a missive to the Citizens of the future. It was the aspiration of our prudent progenitors that this illuminating approximation we call Ironclad was first fired off into our newest Centurial. Congratulations Citizens! Generations have dedicated themselves to this righteous illuminating cause!

Behold: these masterpieces of a forgotten era!

As said by She, the Prophet She: *In the Flames of Progress, eventually, even aging will be optional.*

& don't we all wish to read the mind of a god, in particular—an essential spirit, a god burning without a name.

For the purposes of compiling a definitive narrative we have omitted many of the fragments unearthed from the geological strata that hold no clear expression of reason or emotion.

As has been alluded to in the mass media, et al., there are some curious circumstances involved in this excavation, which has continued faithfully in those capable hands of several generations of archeologists & smiths & metaphysicians who stand before you in the here & now. I urge you to ignore these untruths. They are but commonplace opinions from small minds.

How many resets of probable memory are needed for our universe to build herself into her intended cosmic wondrousness?

[•••] *Elucidation*

Most of you outside Trottelheim will realize that the sequential mythology in this singular anthology of fragments & anointed texts have been laid out by She, in Her prophetic & bounteous *Immaculate Book of Slag*. Even if you are an Unbeliever, as I am, you will be familiar with the narrative of Ø & her magickal, mycelium-infused toes from which emerged the gnarled roots of the great city. In this Ironclad library of human history, some of the questions we have asked are these:

204

How much would historical perspective alter given these newly uncovered evidences?

Do we judge the blessed texts on their logic, or upon metaphysical inquiry alone?

Clearly civilization & civilizing are strange bedfellows, & the latter is an enigmatic property passed on unevenly.

The Prophet has divined the path of all societies, & the Great Circle shall return into her fecund eternity within the Flames of Elucidation.

Solid objects solidify a sense of reality by providing material evidence. But might we not go from one piece of evidence to another, based on a historical record that we constructed rather than one that existed prior to said reconstruction?

(It would also be possible just to move from one piece of evidence to another & thereby form an antecedent for what ensues, but in essence this would be tailoring the evidence to meet the story. & yet, there would still be so many apparent supports to the proposed history. Are we just using these 'clues' to justify our own role in the historical record?)

This too is the archeology of the human mind expressed in pictures that mean sounds.

Surely there are reasons there are ancient stories, & they are not necessarily all historical. How many of you remember who your great-great grandparents were & who they were in the scheme of the narrative? Why, I ask you, are we so unfamiliar with our own past? Is human memory limited only to the few generations before?

Perhaps the rest is embedded in a mythological & genealogical mystery? What have we remembered from our ancestors? & what precisely did they pass on to us other than their inherited genes? & do these genes remember states from the past & adapt them for the future?

History is the scientific enquiry into the past; & yet, is it not mythology that builds the foundation of culture? The journey, of course, is deep inside, one without physical form.

As She, the Prophet She, once said: *Who doesn't want to be an ascetic? It is only in the absence of worldly pleasures that the mind bridges the gaps between life & Otherlife. Even if traumatizing, who doesn't want to have dialogues with their creator?*

But when you return from the space journey & you have hands, do you remember your own name? & does the past have true power, or is it causal? Or is consciousness actually just the present moment?

In these cultural symbols, which become language, layers of meaning & context remain hidden in the cultural collective of memory: to deny the future one fails in the present.

I wonder if any of them believed they saw the future.

May your Otherlife be prosperous & blossom, Citizen.

A Few Words from *Her Immaculate Book of Slag*

*From a version officially endorsed by
the Daughters of the Second Revolution*

It is Fire
that permits
the hand
to enter
the Flame.

— Furioso Ecphrasictus, *Annals of the Iron Prophets*

The Alembic

Psalm 1, Verse for the Anointed

Consumed by the fires of sulfuric desire,
then consummated by a transient, transtidal

blood-flushing, a rage & a rising-falling,
a psychic smoldering-clamoring

for further heavy-breathing, &/or the-ardor-of-
the-internal-combustion-engine; & then

that bubbling-festering that metastatically
infuses ironstone, coke & limestone.

& in the hot, spitting metalloids
who enflame the Iron Heart of Ore,

those blind precious metals briefly leaching
in the glowing Pain of Rebirth.

Mirroring the Perfection of the Heavens

Psalm II, Verse for the Mummified

Where the Word is but the name
of the One, is the Rose, but also

the Thorn; where a beggar squats
on every corner for edible alms, or

a mouse scours attics & drains;
where spaces fill up in the overflow—

then, that brief contiguous spark,
& the flash of Her Fire on wood, & in Her

210

furious, furious, flammable equivocations.

The Song of Her Heavy Fire

Psalm III, Verse for the Transmuted

Listen, dear echoes, to the heart
of her eternally burning flame.

Listen to the crack of her ligneous core,
the static of water churning into hot steam.

& listen to her bellow her billowing blowholes
discharging hot matter & cooling ash

into the Immutable Fueling
of the Great Chain of Being & Becoming.

Fire & Song are
mistresses of Consciousness.

—She, the Prophet, She

The Illustrations

Artifacts illustrated by the Iron Plier Society's commissioned sketch artist, Germonia Smythe-Hardiman. meta.

The archaic Proto-Ossetian idiom & the metaphorical, almost volatile, nature of a significant number of the texts present a serious challenge to their translator-philologists. The outcome of the translation process is often heavily influenced by external inference concerning the writings' actual purpose. The information in the light is that which is not actually seen.

J3761-A: Translation on a silver amulet wrapped around a female pointer and middle fingers

215

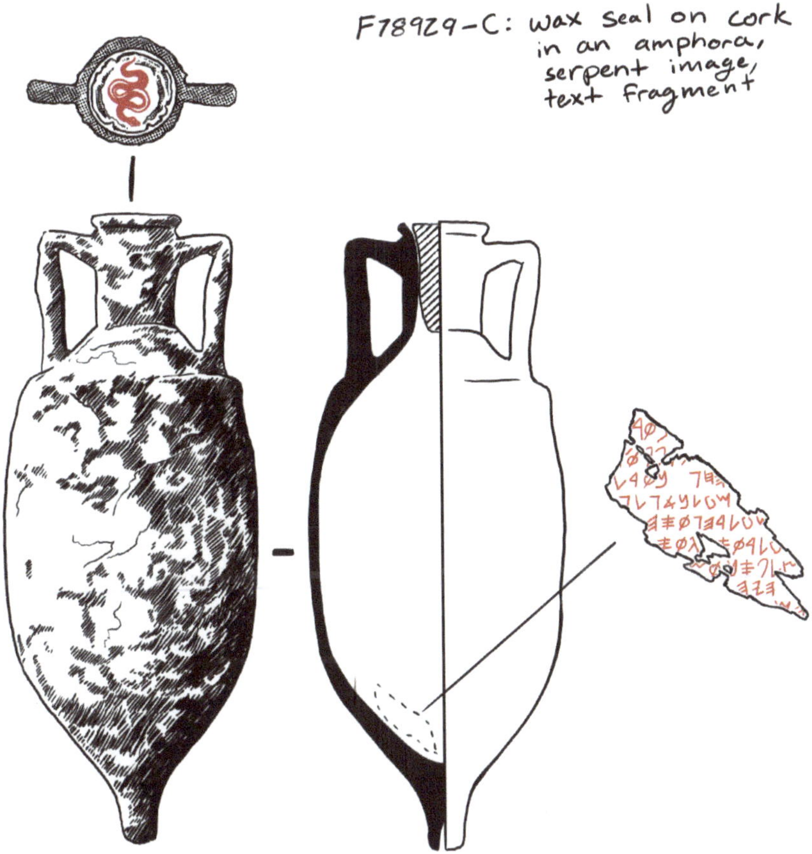

F78929-C: wax seal on cork
in an amphora,
serpent image,
text fragment

217

J 1159 - C : Graffiti on marble
tomb stone

D1877A — B : Inscription on the broken
D1877B — B   stem of an ornamental
             scale. Metal crest of snake
             and sun found in adjacent
             pit

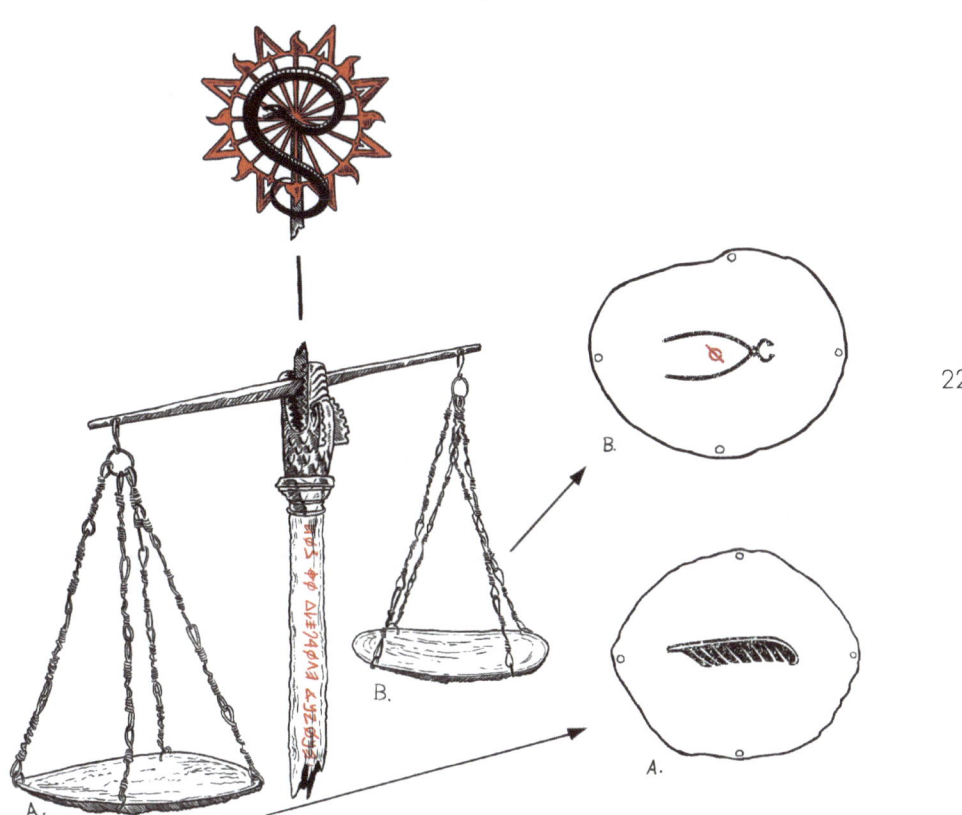

221

F77-B : Broken sun sceptre,
words etched in handle

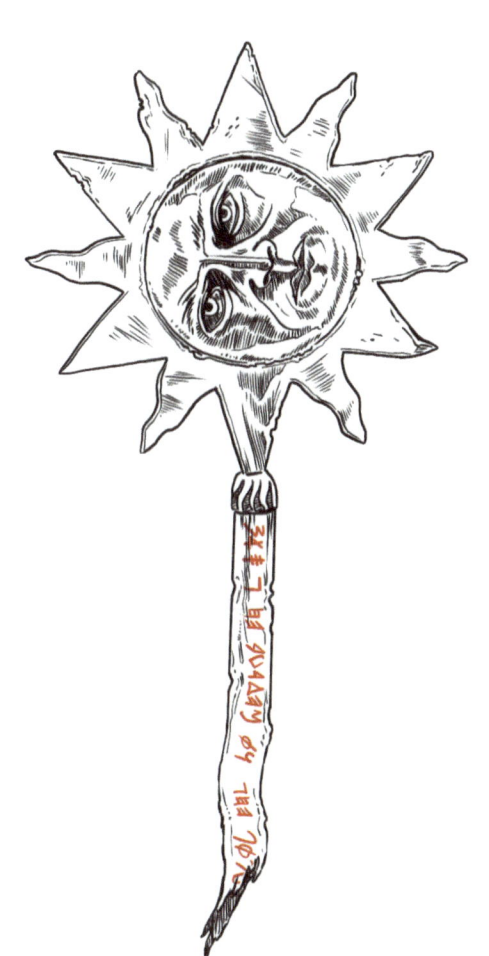

223

F3557-B: Fresco fragment from
a tavern in Magenticum

C1039 - E: Two fragments wrapped around a human tibia

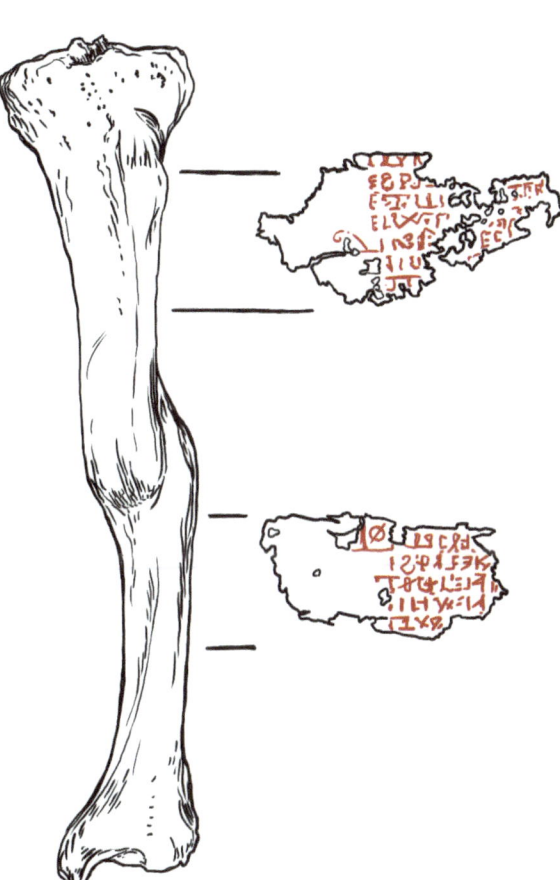

227

D4415-E: Fossilized mechanical
device, with grafitti

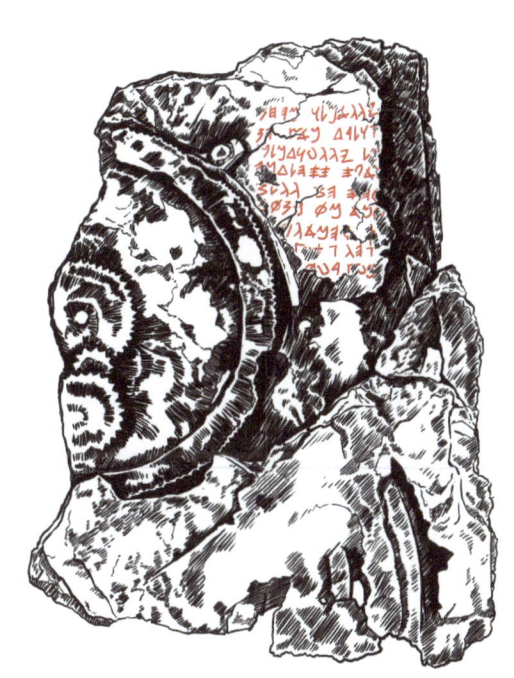

AZ15 - A: Broken wax seal,
tooth marks

231

C103955-E: Four word inscription on the fossilized eye of a praying mantis

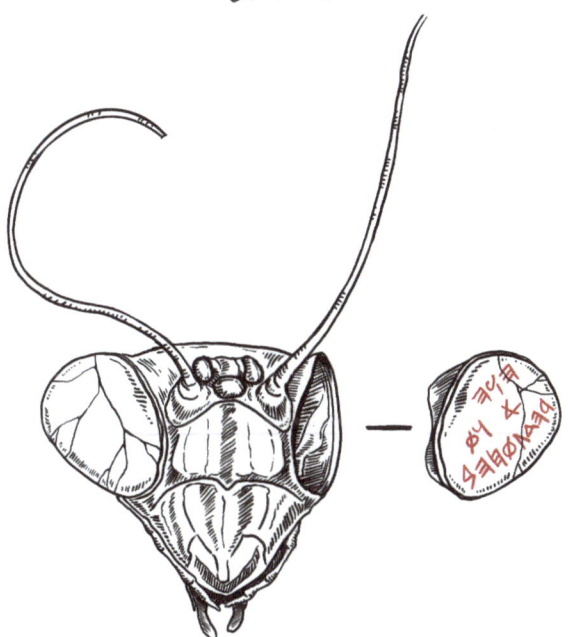

A8812-B : Marble coffin fragment, graffiti:

A 2215—C: Fresco Fragment from a
bordello in Ossetia

237

Referenced Books & Sources

She, The Prophet, She. *Her Immaculate Book of Slag* (City of New Ø: The Iron Plier Society Press)

Anon. *The Gilded Letters of the Prophet* (New Netherlandia: Utopia University Press, ⊙•⊙⊙⊙•••)80Iv•

Anon. *An Anonymous Prophet & Her Seven Sins* (Severania: University of Archenheim Press, ⊙•⊙⊙⊙••)27v•Livia

Anon. *The Cyclical Nature of Augmented Proto-Reality* (New Netherlandia: Utopia University Press, ⊙•⊙⊙⊙•••)i-1v•

Anon. *Daughters of Suns: Some Unpublished Letters of the Prophet, with an Introduction & Commentary, by Jean-Paul Flysson-Sasson* (Black Hand Society Contextual Editions, New Ossetia Branch, ⊙⊙⊙••⊙)

Abydon-Festerman, Sulian. cs. *The Pinwheel of Time. Ladderfish behavior in Context: An Undoing* (West Ossetia B: Foundry Press ⊙•⊙⊙⊙••••⊙)7v•

Alion, Hermeticus., meta. *Gnarled Roots: The Seventy Years War & Her Despots & Dictators (How the Myth Survives)* (West Ossetia B: Foundry Press, ⊙⊙•⊙⊙•)17v•

Busun Hua Xing. *The Long Common Era: An Exploration of the Allusions of Civilized Society in Ritual Context* (Black Hand Society Contextual Editions, Trottelheim Branch, ⊙⊙⊙⊙•••)

Bang-Flysson, Rapangi. *Seven Fire Horses: Quantum Mechanics & the Astral Plane of Understanding* (Trottelheim Zwei: Eisen Editions, ⊙⊙•⊙⊙)

Dadelus, Convecto. alch. *Mirroring the Perfection of the Heavens*, trans. from the ancient Ossetian Linear B2 by Irregula Flysson-Smythe, cs. (West Ossetia B: Foundry Press, ⊙•⊙⊙⊙•••)3v•

Ecphrasictus, Furioso, alch. *On the Nature of Consciousness & Other Inorganic Matters*, trans. from the ancient Ossetian Linear B2 by Irregula Flysson-Smythe, cs. (West Ossetia B: Foundry Press, ⊙•⊙⊙⊙••)19v•

Eisenbein-Flysson, Diamond. *Serpents & Sages: Relevance in the Metaphor within the Myth* (Trottelheim Zwei: Eisen Editions, ⊙•⊙⊙••••)81rev••

Eisenbein, Jared. *Mother Oil & Grandmother Sun: A Study in Contextual Archetypes* (City of New ∅: Copperwood Federal Reserve Press, ⊙•⊙⊙⊙••)1v

Epson-Flysson, Jerry, sr. sg. *Layered Meanings: Geological Strata & the Archeological Record in New ∅* (City of New ∅: The Archetype Book Society, ⊙•⊙••••)22v

Faustina, Illyria, sg. *7000 Years of Civil Serpents* (Trottelheim Zwei: Eisen Editions, ⊙•••⊙⊙•)7bv••

Faustina, Illyria. sg. *Two Ravens Fly like a Serpent: Myth & Movements in a Linear Narrative.* (City of New ∅: *The Journal of Iron Culture & Practical Knowledge*, ⊙••⊙⊙•)3v•rev, vols. 3, 4 & 17

Faustina-Eisenbein, Antonius. *Anaroxis: A Spume of Creation. An Intertextual Analysis* (City of New ∅: *The Journal of Iron Culture & Practical Knowledge*, ⊙••⊙⊙••••)7v•rev, vols. 22, 7 & 3

Faustina- Einsenbein, Severus. meta. *Hungry Daemons: How Myth Created Almost Everything* (New Ossetia: The Beyond Center⊙•⊙••⊙⊙••)1v

Faustina-Flysson, Fredericka. meta. *Carbon Derivatives, Fiery Indices & Other So-Called Cyptocurrencies* (Trottelheim Zwei: University Press Two, ⊙•⊙⊙⊙•••)

Flysson-Mussoud, Starchild. cs. *How the Story Begins: An Iconologistist's View* (Trottelheim Zwei: Eisen Editions, ⊙•⊙⊙⊙•)22rev••

Flysson-Sasson, Jean-Paul. meta. *A Small Carbon Footprint with Ancient Prophets & Sages* (New Netherlandia: Utopia University Press, ⊙•⊙⊙⊙•)2rev•

Flysson-Sasson, Jean-Paul. meta. *Better the Daemon You Know: An Unlocked Code in the Ancient Genome* (New Netherlandia: Utopia University Press, ⊙•••⊙⊙•)fst•

Flysson-Sasson, Jean-Paul. meta. *Hypotheses of Lost Civilizations: Portable & Parietal Art: A Testament on the Cellular Level* (New Netherlandia: Utopia University Press, ⊙••⊙⊙⊙••)2v•

Flysson-Smythe, Genara. *A Brief Study of the Moonpeoples & their Cryptofingers* (lecture given at the New Ø Philological Society under the auspices of the Black Hand Society, ⊙⊙⊙⊙••)

Flysson-Smythe, Inra, cs. *The Divine Serpent Woman in Archeology & Myth* (Eisenheim: Jon, Jon & Jon, ⊙•⊙⊙⊙••••)1.2v•rev

Flysson-Smythe, Inra, cs. *Twisted Tin: A Study in Ancient Metallurgy & its Overarching Effects* (West Ossetia B: Foundry Press ⊙••⊙⊙⊙⊙••⊙)2v•

Flysson-Smythe, Irregula. *Generous Inflections on the State of a Mind: Seven Strata in the New Ossetia* (West Ossetia B: Foundry Press, ⊙•⊙⊙⊙•••)

Flysson-Smythe, Kahlid. meta. *One Thousand & One Writhing Serpents in a Moonbeam: A Synoptic Translation* (lecture presented at The Iron Plier Society, ⊙••⊙••⊙⊙••)

Flysson, Gerome. *Ja Tell Yu Fa: A Philological Excavation with Inherent Biases & Bones. The Subtext within the Subtext* (West Ossetia B: Foundry Press, ⊙•⊙⊙⊙••••⊙)88v•

Fortsetzenheim, Flavia. meta. *Information Structuring Matter: How Myth is Born in Our Mitochondrial Cells* (New Netherlandia: Utopia University Press, ⊙•⊙⊙⊙•)

Goldsmythe-Smythe, Welderen V. cs. meta. *Steering Consciousness for Political Ends: An Overview* (Trottelheim Zwei: University Press Two, ⊙•⊙•⊙•⊙••••)

Goldsmythe-Zanzi, Simon. cs. meta. sg. *Oils of Sanctification* (City of New ∅: Society for the Preservation of Iron & Oil, ⊙•⊙⊙⊙•⊙•)

Goldsmythe-Flysson, Jerome. cs. meta. *A Grand Culture of Nothings: Civilization & its Taming Effects: An Affectation* (New Netherlandia: Black Hand Society Contextual Editions, ⊙⊙••⊙⊙•)

Hardiman, Ezia, meta. *A Hard Alchemy of Tin & Iron & Oil, & the Unfortunate Fruits of Eisenheim* (Eisenheim: Jon, Jon & Jon, ⊙•⊙⊙⊙••)1.8v•rev

242 Hardiman-Flysson, Jerome. meta. *Volcanism & the Origin of the World* (City of New ∅: The Iron Plier Society Press, ⊙⊙⊙••⊙⊙⊙••)97v• rev••

Hardiman-Zenos, Wulan. *Understated Circumstances: How Seven Generations Uncovered the World Before the Flysson* (City of New ∅: The Iron Plier Society Press, ⊙•⊙•⊙⊙••)

Ironsdottir-Smythe, Zeeman. ss. *The Heart Is a Lie: A History of the Soul* (City of New O: The Archetype Book Society, ⊙•⊙•⊙•⊙••)2v• rev

Ironsdottir-Smythe, Zeeman. ss. *Absence in Absentia: More Moon than Dog* (Trottelheim Zwei: University Press Two, ⊙•⊙•⊙•⊙•)

Ironsson-Smythe, Undula. ss. *Up-Down Agriculture & the Daughters of the Second Revolution* (lecture presented to the Iron Plier Society under the auspices of the Black Hand Society, ⊙•⊙•⊙•⊙••••)

Ironsson-Smythe, Undula. ss. *Geochemical signatures of the teeth & micro-traces of behavior in the fossil record* (City of New Ø: *The Journal of Iron Culture & Practical Knowledge*, ⊙••⊙⊙•)5v•rev, vols. 3 & 5

Ironsson-Smythe, Undula. ss. *How a Turtle Survived the Fish & the Sea: Residue of the Last Great Extinction* (City of New Ø: *The Journal of Iron Culture & Practical Knowledge*, ⊙••⊙⊙•)7v•rev, vols. 1 & 3

Juliran, Zakatosh. *Volcanism & Ancient Earthworks* (Black Hand Society Contextual Editions, Trottelheim Branch, ⊙⊙⊙⊙•••)

Juliran, Zakatosh. *Entropic Phenomena: Believing is Mostly Seeing* (New Netherlandia: Utopia University Press, ⊙•⊙⊙•)fst•

Juliran-Hardiman, Snella. *More so than Not: Defining the World by the Sun* (City of New Ø: The Archetype Book Society, ⊙•⊙⊙⊙⊙••)ii

Juliran-Hardiman, Snella. *A Vestibule in the Sun. Sacred Tongs, Ravens, & an Exceptionally Clever Octopus* (City of New Ø:The Archetype Book Society, ⊙•⊙⊙⊙•••)lv

Juliran-Flysson. Henrietta. *How ⊘ means More than ⊘. Another Way of Looking at the Cyclical Nature of Things* (Eisenheim: Jon, Jon & Jon, ⊙••⊙⊙•⊙••)

Khan-Smythe-Flysson. Alexis. alch. *Practical Occultism: From the Private Letters of a Prophet* (City of New Ø:The Archetype Book Society, ⊙•⊙⊙••••)3v•

Khan-Smythe-Flysson. Alexis. alch. *Deep in the Lower Strata: Redeeming Culture in the Dirt* (Trottelheim:Trottel Books, ⊙•⊙•⊙••••)8v•

Khan-Smythe-Flysson. Zuma. cs. alch. *Pseudo-Archeology for Dummies*, 7th Edition (Trottelheim:Trottel Books, ⊙•⊙•⊙•••)7v•

Leeman-Smythe-Hardiman, Jennifer. *Iron Hands: A Reflection on Metallurgy in the Coarse Historical Context* (City of New Ø: The Iron Plier Society Press, ⊙•⊙•⊙•••••)

Macron-Smythe, Ironside. *A Common Ancestor before the Deluge: On the Writings of Furioso Ecphrasictus* (City of New Ø: The Journal of Iron Culture & Practical Knowledge, ⊙••⊙⊙⊙•••)2v•rev, vols. 2 & 21

Mushu, Zaphilia. *Motherblood Volcanism in All Her Fiery Mercies: An Exogenesis of Seven Cities Spared the Great Exfoliation* (Ossetia B: Archenheim Press, ⊙•⊙⊙⊙⊙•••)Iv•

Mushu-Smythe, Gerald. meta. *How Fire Created Almost Everything: A Study in Kind* (Suverania: Iron Egg Books, ⊙⊙••⊙⊙••)

Mushu-Smythe, Illuria. ss. *Foraging versus Farming: The Hive Mind* (City of New Ø: Society for the Preservation of Iron & Oil, ⊙⊙⊙•••⊙⊙•)

244   Paraplaxis, Querilla. alch. *She, the Prophet, She Sings of Fire*, trans. from the ancient Ossetian Linear B2 by Gerome Flysson (City of New Ø: The Iron Plier Society Press, ⊙•⊙••⊙⊙⊙) div•

Paraplaxis, Querilla. alch. *Her Immaculate Book of Slag: Letters & Correspondences: Alchemists, Metaphysicians, Smiths, & Sages* (West Ossetia B: Foundry Press, ⊙•⊙⊙⊙•••)8v•

Paraplaxis, Querilla. alch. *The Calligraphy of the Serpent through Linear Time*, trans. from the ancient Ossetian Linear B2 by Gerome Flysson (City of New Ø: The Iron Plier Society Press, ⊙•⊙•⊙⊙••••)div•

Patchu-Pan, Squirrel. *Alternative Interpretations of Consciousness: How the World Became Real* (City of New Ø: The Archetype Book Society, ⊙•⊙⊙⊙•••)Iv

Que-Smythe, XingLing. cs, meta. *Seventeen Moons in the Habitable Zone. A Study in Alternative Origin Hypotheses* (Trottelheim: Trottel Books, ⊙•⊙•⊙••)7v•

Quelesteria, Monoxis. alch. *Beyond Life & Alchemy: Seven Geofractal Immigrations That Defined Civilization* (Ossetia B: Archenheim Press, ⊙•⊙⊙⊙⊙•)33v•

Rastavulen, Heremon. *The Unknown in the Geological Record* (Black Hand Society Contextual Editions, New-Ossetia Branch, ⊙⊙⊙•⊙••••)

Reed-Flysson, Tongo. cs. alch. *Geoglyphs of the Rainforest* (Ossetia B: Archenheim Press, ⊙⊙•⊙⊙⊙••)iiv•

Smythe-Flysson, JaJa Long. *However Hungry the World Becomes: Carbon Derivatives, Fiery Indices, & Further So-Called Cyptocurrencies* (Trottelheim: Trottel Books, ⊙•⊙⊙⊙•••)5,4v••

Smythe-Hardiman, Moon. *Once Where Wind Was Born. A Study in Breath & Firebreathing* (West Ossetia B: Foundry Press, ⊙⊙⊙•••⊙•)v-x•

Smythe-Hardiman, Moon. *Tidal Forces, Wormholes & Mining Techniques in a Revised Context* (West Ossetia B: Foundry Press, ⊙⊙⊙••••⊙•••)v-xi•

Smythe-Hardiman, Moon. *Where Worlds Collide: As Below, So Above* (West Ossetia B: Foundry Press, ⊙⊙⊙••••⊙••)i-xii•

Smythe-Mabuti, Zafu. alch. *Dynamics of the Psychic World* (Trottelheim: Trottel Books, ⊙•⊙•⊙••)•

Smythe-Pluteron, Vessia. cs. alch. *The Esoteric Tradition & The Physics of The Secret Doctrine* (Suverania: Iron Egg Books, ⊙•⊙•⊙•)

Smythe-Listerman, Yanos. cs. *A Sandwich Somewhere Near the End of Time. An Anthropomorphic Approach to Legend & Myth* (City of New ∅: Society for the Preservation of Iron & Oil, ⊙•⊙⊙⊙••)

Smythe-Listerman, Yanos. cs. *Fragmentary Evidence: The Lost City of ∅ & the Federal Copperwood Industry* (City of New ∅: Society for the Preservation of Iron & Oil, ⊙•⊙⊙⊙⊙)2.7v•rev

Smythe,Ying, Simone. *Linear Narratives in a Derivative State* (West Ossetia B: Foundry Press, ⊙•••⊙••••)12v•

Smythe-Ying-Simone. cs. *Chemical Signatures of Sediment Layers & Their Topographical Histories & the Fossil Record* (West Ossetia B: Foundry Press, ⊙•••⊙••)3v•

Suveran-Hardiman-Flysson, Ilya. *A Life & a Year in Trottelheim in Ancient Context* (Trottelheim: Trottel Books, ⊙•⊙⊙⊙•••)5,4v••

Suveran-Hardiman-Flysson, Ilya. *A Mystical Accord: Daemons, Dignitaries & Dictators* (Trottelheim: Trottel Books, ⊙•••⊙••⊙•••)1v•

Telleman-Hardiman-Flysson, Binya. *Tears of Mercy: How the Ancient World Made the Modern World* (New Netherlandia: Utopia University Press, ⊙•⊙••••⊙•)gg•

Tungut, Shashamal. *Motherblood: Foundation Myths, Forbidden Numerology, the Equinox & the Agricultural Calendar* (Suverania: Iron Egg Books, ⊙•⊙⊙•)

Venison-Hardiman, Peabody. meta. *Fur, Skins, & Other Telltale Evidence of an Advanced Civilization Before the Deluge* (Tellamon Books & Paraphenalia, ⊙⊙•⊙⊙••••)iv

Xirxies-Smythe, Julia. cs, meta. *Narratives in Forbidden Literature* (West Ossetia B: Foundry Press, ⊙⊙•⊙⊙•) vol3•

YY-Ya. *Selfish Genes & Foreign Fowl. Across the Border of Delights: How Agriculture Begins in Its Earliest Form* (Suverania: Iron Egg Books, ⊙•⊙⊙•••)

YingLa-Smythe & B. Festermann, Yuri. *Mushroom of Souls: A Brief Encounter with Sentient Others* (City of New ∅: Society for the Preservation of Iron & Oil, ⊙•⊙⊙⊙⊙••••)1•rev

YingLa-Smythe & B. Festermann, Yuri. *Pseudo-archaeology & Her Other Fringe Paleontological Pursuits* (Severania: University of Archenheim Press, ☉•☉☉☉☉••)53v•Hermetica

Zenos, Adolfo-Generalissimo. cs. meta. *Mucosal Movements in a Dark Continent: A Colloquial Study of Wall Carvings* (City of New Ø: Society for the Preservation of Iron & Oil, ☉•☉☉☉•☉•)

Zenos-Smythe, Fortunato. alch. meta. *Fragmentary Evidence: How Timing Effects Everything* (New Netherlandia: Utopia University Press, ☉•☉☉☉••)ivi•

We would like to thank the Society for the Preservation of Iron & Oil, the Society of Iron Culture & Practical Understanding, Trottelheim Zwei: University Press Two, & Iron Alchemy Journal for their continued support & understanding during these hard times. A selection of these books & journals are available through the Irønclad Museum bookstore.

The Author and the Illustrator

Marc Vincenz is a multilingual translator, poet, fiction writer, journalist, editor, musician and artist. He has published many books of poetry, fiction and translation. His recent poetry collections include *The Pearl Diver of Irunmani, A Splash of Cave Paint, The King of Prussia is Drunk on Stars, Faery Ecology*, and forthcoming in 2026 from White Pine Press, *No More Animal Poems*. His translation of award-winning Swiss poet and novelist, Klaus Merz' selected poems, *An Audible Blue*, won the 2023 Massachusetts Book Award for Translated Literature. He translates from the German, Romanian, French and Spanish.

Jake Quatt is a multi-disciplinary artist based in Minneapolis currently working in illustration, printmaking, animation, and shadow puppetry. Jake received his B.A in Fine Arts and Journalism from Beloit College in 2019 and moved to Minneapolis in early 2020. He currently illustrates for MadHat Press, Unlikely Books, and Spuyten Duyvil, animates for the Science Museum of Minnesota, and puppeteers with The Heart of the Beast Theatre. He is currently collaborating with Marc Vincenz on a graphic novel entitled *Coalition No. 9*. He can be found on Instagram @ jake_quatt_arts.

Other Books by the Author

Poetry

The Propaganda Factory, or Speaking of Trees

Mao's Mole

Gods of a Ransacked Century

Behind the Wall at the Sugar Works (a verse novel)

Beautiful Rush

Additional Breathing Exercises (bilingual German and English)

This Wasted Land and Its Chymical Illuminations (annotated by Tom Bradley)

Becoming the Sound of Bees

Sibylline (illustrated by Dennis Paul Williams)

The Syndicate of Water & Light

Leaning into the Infinite

Here Comes the Nightdust

Einstein Fledermaus

The Little Book of Earthly Delights

A Brief Conversation with Consciousness (illustrated by Sophia Santos)

There Might Be a Moon or a Dog

39 Wonders and Other Management Issues

The Pearl Diver of Irunmani

A Splash of Cave Paint

The King of Prussia is Drunk on Stars

All the Tricks of Language

No More Animal Poems

Mythodology

The Form of Time: New and Selected Poems

Spells for the Wicked (illustrated by Sophia Santos and Jake Quatt)

Limited Editions and Chapbooks

Benny and the Scottish Blues (illustrated by Darene Dewan)
Genetic Fires
Upholding Half the Sky
Pull of the Gravitons
An Alphabet of Last Rites
Thieves' Canto
The Mayfly Codex
Three Telltale Love Signs
Rocketship to the Andromeda Galaxy
Faery Ecology (illustrated by Sophia Santos)

Translations

Kissing Nests by Werner Lutz
Nightshift / An Area of Shadows by Erika Burkart and Ernst Halter
A Late Recognition of the Signs by Erika Burkart
Grass Grows Inward by Andreas Neeser
Out of the Dust by Klaus Merz
Secret Letter by Erika Burkart
Lifelong Bird Migration by Jürg Amann
Unexpected Development by Klaus Merz
An Audible Blue: Selected Poems (1963–2016) by Klaus Merz
Casting a Spell in Spring by Alexander Xaver Gwerder
Country of Small Men by Ernst Halter
In the House, Still Light by Klaus Merz
Mother's Letters: Pure Caviar by Ion Monoran (co-translated with Marius Surleac)
Dreaming Jack by Klaus Merz

Fiction

The Visitation
Three Taos of Tao, or How to Catch a Fortuitous Elephant
City of Lemons (illustrated by Sophia Santos)

Graphic Novel

Coalition No. 9 (illustrated by Jake Quatt)

CIAO

At once archaeology, geology, and alchemy, *Ironclad* delves into human memory, precisely that memory of things that never quite were. The Biblical expression, בכתכ, *as it is written*, resonates throughout this intricate cast-iron lacery of the sacred, the mythical, the primordial, somehow unfrozen and revived by the poet's molten ink. I enjoin all readers in search of poetry to scour these arcane bibliographies. Return always to the moldering and indelible pages of *Her Immaculate Book of Slag*. Return; haunt the strange back streets of the City of Ø, the null-metropolis where nothing lurks, and where, on every empty street corner, no one whispers the forgotten enchantments for which we still yearn.

—Alexander Dickow, author of *Appetites* and *Caramboles*

Marc Vincenz's newest book, *Ironclad*, a novel within a poetry collection plumbing a fictitious archaeological dig, is anything but ironclad. Yet, what is *Ironclad* except conjecture? Or as Vincenz writes, "Rearview reductionism / is what it has been coined." The reader unearths societies, artifacts, histories told through graffiti on the underside of an accountant's iron desk, a dentist's alabaster stool and on a scroll wrapped around a bear's shinbone. Who were they? What did they worship? From where did they come and where did they go? *Ironclad* has the capture of mythic mind and is attuned to recurring global conundrums; pre-diluvian correctionalism, Promethean transference, modern absurdity…, how to be a part and apart?

As the novel's archeologist digs, you, reader, are gifted a spade. Conjure.

—Aby Kaupang, author of & *there's you still thrill hour of the world to love*

www.ingramcontent.com/pod-product-compliance
Lightning Source LLC
Chambersburg PA
CBHW041452120626
46547CB00003B/427